I0813799

UNION PACIFIC

and Its Predecessors

BRIAN SOLOMON

Kalmbach Media

Dedication

In memory of Jim Wrinn, editor of *Trains* (2004-2022), who inspired a generation of Union Pacific enthusiasts.

Acknowledgements

This book is the culmination of more than 30 years of research and collective experience with Union Pacific that wouldn't have been possible without the help of many people along the way. Fellow photographers and students of railroad history, technology, and operation with whom I traveled during my explorations of the railroad contributed greatly to my education, appreciation, and understanding of the UP and its components. These include: Brian Jennison, J.D. Schmid, Vic Neves, Dave Stanley, Brian Rutherford, Bob Morris, Brad Hellman, Jon Roma, Mike Abalos, Mel Patrick, T.S. Hoover, Tom Danneman, Mike Danneman, John Gruber, Rich Gruber, Dan Munson, Travis Berryman, Joe McMillan, Dave Burton, Don Marson, Howard Ande, Dean Sauvola, Chris Guss, Marshall Beecher, Mark Hemphill, Blair Kooistra, David Hegarty, Gerald Hook, Phil Brahms, Justin Tognetti, and Brian Schmidt. Over the years I interviewed many people knowledgeable of matters relating to Western and Midwestern railroading, including Richard Steinheimer, Dick Dorn, Mike Blaszak, Gordon Glattenberg, Doug Harrop, Phil Gosney, Dale Sanders, Mike Schafer, Jim Boyd, Wayne Monger, and Ed Burkhardt. Thanks to the members of the Irish Railway Record Society in Dublin, where I spent countless hours procuring information. Thanks to Kurt Bell at the Railroad Museum of Pennsylvania; to Union Pacific's Bill Kratville and John Bromley; to Southern Pacific's Bob Hoppe, Bart Nadeau, and John Signor; to California State Railroad Museum's Walter Gray and Paul Hammond; to the members of the Golden Gate Railway Museum; to members of Western Railway Museum at Rio Vista, California; and Scott Lothes of the Center for Railroad Photography & Art. Thanks to all the photographers and archives that supplied illustrations considered for this project. Special thanks are due to my editor at Kalmbach, Jeff Wilson; my father, Richard Jay Solomon, who provided source materials and illustrations and helped proofread the text; and my fiancée Kris Sabbatino, who encouraged me during the writing process.

— Brian Solomon, September 2022

Kalmbach Media
21027 Crossroads Circle
Waukesha, Wisconsin 53186
www.KalmbachHobbyStore.com

© 2023 Brian Solomon
All rights reserved. This book may not be reproduced in part or in whole by any means whether electronic or otherwise without written permission of the publisher except for brief excerpts for review.

Published in 2023
27 26 25 24 23 1 2 3 4 5

Manufactured in China

ISBN: 978-162700-926-3
EISBN: 978-162700-927-0

Editor: Jeff Wilson
Book Design: Lisa Bergman

Library of Congress Control Number: 2022945977

On the cover: This view through a concrete snow shed shows an eastbound empty coal train (right) passing a manifest freight at West Norden, Calif., on Dec. 5, 2020. *T.S. Hoover*

Back cover: Union Pacific SD9043MAC No. 8256 leads a pair of former Southern Pacific AC4400CWs on an eastbound train of Powder River coal east of Lusk, Wyo., on Oct. 12, 2003. *Jeff Wilson*

CONTENTS

The U50 was General Electric's initial double-diesel offering. The unique-to-the-UP locomotive was essentially two U25Bs on a long frame under one hood and controlled by a single throttle.
General Electric

UP UNDER CLEAR WESTERN SKIES

When I was young, Union Pacific was an abstract distant railroad that represented the optimism of clear Western skies that I knew only through photos. I was fascinated by UP's 1930s streamliners, their gaping front grilles that looked like enormous mouths that captured my imagination as wondrous examples of passenger trains from another era. As a teenager, I was inspired by a UP promotional film on its famed Northern (4-8-4) steam locomotive No. 8444 (before it was renumbered back to 844), which brought to life this amazing machine in all of its technological perfection.

My first real impression of Union Pacific was driving west to live in California in 1989. Robert A. Buck, a UP fan and proprietor of Tucker's Hobbies in Warren, Mass., suggested I follow U.S. 30 across Nebraska, which ran parallel to UP's double-track main line. With this in mind I drove west, intersecting the Chicago & North Western east-west main line at Marshalltown, Iowa, and followed the tracks from there. At Boone, Iowa, I visited the Boone & Scenic Valley tourist line where I was invited for a ride on one of their electrics. When I explained where I was headed, they said, "Wow, you're in luck! Union Pacific is running 844 on a freight west from Omaha tomorrow!"

I arrived in Fremont, Neb., early in the morning of September 24 and followed the famous transcon westward under clear skies and was awed by the continuous parade of freights along the Overland Route. Near Duncan, Neb., I saw my first modern wide-cab diesel, a new SD60M. I paced a westbound American President Lines double-stack train from Silver Creek to Central City, Neb., noting that it kept rolling along at a steady 50 mph. East of Grand Island, Neb., I picked a spot and waited, wondering if my friends in Boone had sent me on a goose chase. After a while I spotted wafts of dark exhaust on the eastern horizon, and at 12:36 pm the majestic locomotive came into view. There was UP's last steam locomotive, No. 844, leading a short freight with a Missouri Pacific caboose at the rear. For the next four hours, I followed this marvelous locomotive, making photos along the way.

My most vivid memory was west of Kearney, Neb. To stay ahead of the steam

Catching UP No. 844 working a freight train unassisted was an enormous thrill. On Sept. 25, 1989, the 4-8-4 works west on Archer Hill on its way to Cheyenne, Wyo. *Brian Solomon*

Sunrise on June 9, 1996 finds an eastbound Union Pacific freight rolling across Chicago & North Western's landmark Kate Shelley High Bridge over the Des Moines River west of Boone, Iowa. Completed in 1901, it replaced the older low-level structure where young Kate Shelley warned a train of a washout during a storm. In 2009, UP opened a modern bridge alongside this structure. *Brian Solomon*

locomotive, I was driving west on U.S. 30 as fast as I dared in my white Toyota Corolla, only to see the locomotive bearing down on me in my rearview mirror! This 1944-built Alco 4-8-4 with freight train in tow overtook my racing Toyota effortlessly. Not long after, No. 844 had to slow when it caught the approach signals from another westbound freight ahead. At North Platte, I drove to the visitor's center at the famous Bailey Yard. This vast yard was filled with freight cars and movement everywhere. Watching No. 844 glide along modern diesels in the yard seemed incongruous, yet welcome.

At North Platte I learned that UP was going to repeat the steam freight exercise the following day, as No. 844 was needed in Cheyenne, Wyo. I continued west on U.S.

In July 2005, GE AC4400CW No. 5922 (UP class C44AC-CTE) leads an eastbound freight toward Donner Summit, passing the rim of the American River Canyon east of Alta, Calif., near the old SP timetable location appropriately called "Gorge." *Brian Solomon*

30 and took a motel near Ogallala, Neb., to resume my exploration of UP's main line in the morning. At daybreak I enjoyed another morning of cloudless blue skies. Following the railroad west, I visited Chappell, Sidney, and Kimball, Neb., photographing long freights everywhere I stopped. At 10:59 a.m. I crossed the Wyoming state line. In 6 hours, I'd seen a dozen freights. At 2:33 p.m., I was in Hillsdale, Wyo., when No. 844 caught up with me again, this time leading an empty hopper train. An hour later I arrived in Cheyenne. My first two days watching UP set the stage for my further explorations of the railroad over the next two decades.

While living in northern California, I explored UP's former Western Pacific, especially in the rocky confines of the Feather River Canyon. I invested lots of time exploring the Southern Pacific before it merged with UP in 1996. I made trips to explore UP's grades in eastern Oregon where the railroad crosses Encina and Telocaset Hills and crests again at Kamela Summit in the Blue Mountains. I visited California's Cajon Pass and the moon-like Afton Canyon. In the mid-1990s, fellow photographer Mel Patrick and I made memorable trips along the Los Angeles & Salt Lake route, exploring obscure locations on the Western Pacific in the Utah and Nevada deserts and along the old Denver & Rio Grande Western. Living in Wisconsin, I had made use of ample opportunities to explore Chicago & North Western lines

Union Pacific SD70M No. 4349 works eastbound at milepost 273 near Lebanon, Wis., on the former Chicago & North Western Adams Line—now UP's Adams Subdivision—on Jan. 20, 2019. The route was built by C&NW in the early 20th century as a direct route between Milwaukee and the Twin Cities. *Brian Solomon*

during the time of its merger with UP. In more recent years, I revisited former SP lines now operated by UP, including the famous Donner Pass crossing, the Coast Line in California, and the sinuous route in the Tehachapis. I traveled by Amtrak over the former SP Sunset Route, observed UP operations on the former Missouri Pacific in St. Louis, and followed the former Chicago & Eastern Illinois.

Over the years, I've written about many elements of UP and its predecessors, and accumulated a wide body of research and general understanding. For this book, I've aimed to distill the railroad into those elements that make it what it is today, while focusing on fundamentals of its history and technology that are characteristically Union Pacific. It is neither possible nor desirable to cover the railroad in its entirety. The railroad's long history and extensive operations across its far-flung network could fill—and have filled—volumes. I didn't want this book to read like an old-fashioned phone directory or a catalog. Whenever possible my text provides context to allow understanding why constituents of the railroad came to be, rather than just provide lists of disconnected facts. I've covered some subjects in detail, and necessarily glossed over others.

As I write this in summer 2022, when UP is 160 years old, I wonder what the railroad will be like on its 200th anniversary, and on its 300th!

On July 30, 2016, a trio of new GE Tier 4-compliant ET44AH (UP class C45AH) diesels approach Tunnel 2 on the former Southern Pacific between Bealville and Caliente in the California Tehachapis. When new, UP assigned these low-carbon-emission locomotives to its California main lines. *Brian Solomon*

CHAPTER 1

UNION PACIFIC HISTORY

At more than 160 years, UP is the oldest continually operating major railroad in North America

On Dec. 5, 2020, an eastbound empty coal train passes a waiting manifest as it approaches the cross-over at West Norden, Calif., just shy of the railroad's summit on Donner Pass. The original transcontinental railroad crossing of the Sierra climbs from nearly sea level to an elevation of 6,891 feet in just over 85 miles. A 1980s-era concrete snow shed protects the switches at Norden. *T.S. Hoover*

6794
6794
UNION
PACIFIC

The idea of a transcontinental railroad predated the creation of UP by decades. In the 1840s, railroad visionaries had discussed the possibilities of spanning the continent. Over the years, their ideas inspired the imaginations of builders, businessmen, politicians, and the public.

California dreaming

Prior to the Civil War, Congress investigated several potential rail routes to the West. Plans were political from the start: Southern interests favored a southerly route and northern visionaries plotted more northerly paths. Among the key figures in formative days of transcontinental planning was Grenville Dodge, who in the 1850s conducted preliminary railroad surveys west of the Missouri River and became an early proponent of a Pacific Railway. It is believed that in 1859, when Dodge resided near Council Bluffs, Iowa, he had a fortuitous meeting with presidential candidate Abraham Lincoln and the two men discussed rail routes in the West; they appeared to have agreed that Council Bluffs was ideally situated to launch a Pacific railroad. Dodge joined Lincoln's fledgling Republican Party, supporting his presidential campaign, and Council

In the 1860s, Union Pacific construction crews built track at a feverish pace across the plains and deserts of the West. In the race against Central Pacific, it was more important for UP to build quickly than deliver high quality construction. *Trains collection*

Bluffs was eventually chosen as the eastern terminus for the Pacific Railroad.

During the Civil War, Lincoln's administration viewed the Pacific Railroad as important for the Union to retain control of the West. Because of the strategic nature of this project the central route was selected. The two railroads formed to execute the project were named reflecting the politics of the day: Union Pacific to build west and Central Pacific to build east.

Building a lengthy railroad across unsettled lands—crossing vast distances between population centers—represented a herculean task. Launching the project during a war added complications resulting from the lack of able-bodied men for construction, and the difficulties of attracting investment, not to mention exceptional costs to procure and transport materials.

Following years of discussion and lobbying, President Lincoln signed the Pacific Rail Act on July 2, 1862, authorizing construction and funding for the project. While this act got both Union Pacific and Central Pacific railroads going, it failed to generate necessary private investment to sustain construction, so there was little forward progress during the War. Potential investors in the scheme were discouraged by hundreds of miles of unpopulated, hostile, and barren lands offering little on line traffic between eastern and western terminals. Creative means were required to fund construction.

Union Pacific

On Oct. 29, 1863, 15 months after the Pacific Rail Act was signed, the Union Pacific Railroad was founded with Thomas Durant as its head. He had previously worked on the Chicago & Rock Island and the Missouri & Mississippi, formative lines across the prairies, where he had met key players integral to the early days of UP including Dodge (who would serve as a Union General), John A. Dix, and Peter Dey. Durant served as UP's vice president, and Dix as the line's first president. Dix's prestigious resumé—having served as a U.S. Senator from New York, U.S. Secretary of the Treasury, and president of Missouri & Mississippi—and his Washington connections were valuable in the early days of the UP. Yet, it was Durant who was calling the shots.

Dey was an honest, principled individual, and served as the railroad's first Chief Engineer. He and Dodge located the best route west through the Platte River Valley, but despite this valuable role, Dey had a short career with the Union Pacific. He considered Durant's business practices corrupt and immoral, and resigned his position in protest, with Grenville Dodge assuming the role of Chief Engineer. Durant established company offices in New York City, where he helped create the railroad construction company called the Crédit Mobilier of America.

The Pacific Rail Act of 1862 hadn't established a starting point for the railroad. Omaha and Council Bluffs on opposite sides of the Missouri River offered logical places to begin the westward push. Although not yet connected by rail, both places were easily served by river boat. Omaha was initially the site of public interest. In early

1863, to mark the launch westward, and amidst great fanfare, Nebraska's governor turned a shovelful of earth at Omaha. However, in 1864, UP's official terminus was changed to Council Bluffs. The first rails to the west were not put down for another year and a half, and these arrived by river boat. Connecting railroads from the east reached Council Bluffs only after UP was underway, but a railroad bridge across the Missouri wasn't open until 1872.

The 1862 Act initially didn't encourage sufficient private funding, so CP and UP lobbied the Federal government to sweeten the pot. In 1864, revisions to the Act were introduced that included government bonds to be issued to the railroads for every 20 miles of track completed, enabling the companies to generate necessary funding. These bonds provided short-term cash flow, although the bonds eventually had to be repaid. The railroads also received significant land grants, which included mineral rights that were considerably more generous than those provided by the original 1862 Act.

Building west

Myriad challenges impeded construction in the early years. UP's difficulties, as noted, were complicated by the Civil War, its lack of through railroad connections, and a severe labor shortage. Only in 1865 did the railroad start actively building west. What spurred Union Pacific into action was the clause in the Pacific Rail Act stipulating that if another railroad reached the 100th meridian first, that railroad would be awarded a subsidy for construction instead of UP. So when Kansas Pacific emerged as UP's principal competitor, building westward across Kansas toward Denver, UP reacted by accelerating its tracklaying across Nebraska.

Conclusion of the Civil War freed up thousands of young men looking for work, and by winter 1866 rails had reached North Platte. Yet, slow progress had cost it in

On Oct. 19, 1867, crews lay track on the Kansas Pacific route some 300 miles west of the Missouri River. At the time, KP was confusingly known as the "Union Pacific, Eastern Division" despite having no corporate connection to UP proper. *Union Pacific*

JAY GOULD

Jay Gould was an enigmatic, misunderstood 19th-century financial genius, whose clever manipulations and thorough understanding of the railroad industry gave him the extraordinary power to shape American railroading during one of its most influential periods. On one level, Gould's involvement with Union Pacific was an important stepping stone for his ascendance in American business. On another level, he elevated the company in the wake of the Crédit Mobilier scandal. After blending UP with Kansas Pacific in 1880, he appeared to take his profits from UP as seed money to finance the next stage of his railroad empire building. In rapid succession, Gould bought up a host of marginal railroads, which he transformed into one of the great systems of the 1800s.

Gould created the Missouri Pacific System by melding a host of weak railroads, while completing Texas & Pacific, a key component to MP, and at various times invested in Chicago & North Western, Cotton Belt, Denver & Rio Grande, and Missouri-Kansas-Texas—which would become key components in the late 20th-century UP—as well as controlling railroads elsewhere and building telegraph empires including Western Union. Gould publicly stepped back from Union Pacific in 1884 and installed Charles Francis Adams Jr. as president, only to re-assume control in 1890. When he died two years later his vision was unfulfilled. In the early 1900s Jay's son George built the Western Pacific as an extension of Denver & Rio Grande as part of his transcontinental scheme. One major component of UP's future network that remained largely outside the Goulds' strategy at that time was Southern Pacific.

the race with Central Pacific, which was building eastward. Every mile CP built meant less subsidy for UP, so UP built as fast as its could and by the end of 1867 it reached west of Cheyenne, Wyo., to Sherman Summit. However, it still faced the hard push across difficult terrain to reach the Great Salt Lake. After some tense moments, the building parties of CP and UP agreed on a compromise and settled on Promontory Summit, west of Ogden, Utah, as their formal meeting point. (Afterward, the railroads moved their official interchange to Ogden, with CP assuming control of the line between Ogden and Promontory.)

"Done!"

The railroads used the moment of unification as a media stunt to sell the railroad to the public. Promontory Summit was a desolate site north of the Great Salt Lake. The Golden Spike ceremony was postponed when Vice President Durant's special train was delayed, and the union of UP and CP was marked on May 10, 1869, a day now enshrined in railroad lore. An estimated 600 guests attended, including politicians, railroad officers, soldiers from the 21st Infantry, and the Tenth Ward Headquarters Band. UP's Durant, Dodge, and John "Jack" Casement—the man who was largely responsible for UP's construction—represented the Union Pacific. Central Pacific's Leland Stanford had the honor of placing the final golden spike—18 carats and nearly 6" long bearing the words "The Last Spike."

At 12:47 p.m., a telegrapher relayed a simple message to the world: "Done!"

The effect of the Golden Spike ceremony on the public was akin to the moon landing a century later. The nation had spanned the continent and conquered the wilderness. The world was smaller. Anyone with the money for a train fare could reach California in just a few days without having to endure an epic months-long overland journey. But this wasn't the end: The railroad was hardly complete, and railroad building across the American West had just begun.

World famous Wedding of the Rails: On May 10, 1869, Union Pacific No. 119 (right) met pilot-to-pilot with Central Pacific's *Jupiter* at Promontory Summit, Utah to mark the completion of the transcontinental railroad. In truth, the railroad building had just begun. *Andrew J. Russell, Union Pacific collection*

Union Pacific expansion: Utah branches

UP's early charters restricted it from branchline construction, and for its first 15 years it suffered from a lack of feeders, limiting its ability to generate local traffic. The railroad aggressively expanded its network to tap local traffic and extend its reach.

In its original form, UP's transcontinental route missed two of the largest settlements in the west, Salt Lake City and Denver. Among UP's first feeders was the Utah Central, built by Mormon interests to connect Salt Lake City with the main line at Ogden. UP had invested in this line, which was completed by January 1870, and ultimately took control of it. The UP also funded the Utah Southern, which built southward through the Utah Valley to reach Provo, Utsh, in 1873, and two years later terminated 73 miles south of Salt Lake City at York, Utah. The Utah Northern was more ambitious. It was incorporated by Mormon interests in August 1871 and aimed initially to serve farming communities north of Ogden, but had intentions of tapping lucrative mining camps just over the horizon in southwest Montana. This line, started as three-foot gauge, reached Franklin, Utah, in 1874. Gould encouraged UP to invest in the line, and in 1878 the railroad reorganized it as the Utah & Northern. It built over Monida Pass to reach Butte, Mont., in December 1881 and connected with Northern Pacific at Garrison, Mont., in September, 1883, just a few weeks after NP's northern transcontinental reached the town. In 1887, U&N began converting to standard gauge, and in 1889 it was merged with UP's Oregon Short Line affiliate.

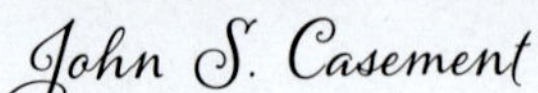

Grenville Mellen Dodge

Oliver Ames

John S. Casement served as a Union Pacific contractor hired in 1866 to build track. His purpose-built construction train pushed westward at an unprecedented rate with his crews laying down three to five miles of track a day.
Union Pacific

Grenville Mellen Dodge was Union Pacific's chief engineer in the 1860s when it made its westward push to meet Central Pacific, a job that made him a national celebrity.
Henry Taylor Jr., Union Pacific collection

Oliver Ames was the director of Crédit Mobilier of America and UP president between 1868 and 1871. His career and health were destroyed by the Crédit Mobilier scandal of the 1870s.
Union Pacific

Kansas Pacific

Kansas Pacific had its origins in the 1850s. In the 1860s, the railroad's promoters adopted the name "Union Pacific, Eastern Division" when they hoped the railroad could become the eastern leg of the Pacific Railroad. Their dream was squelched when UP was the first to reach the 100th meridian. Instead, by 1870 KP connected Kansas City and Denver, where it interchanged with the Denver Pacific Railroad & Telegraph Company. This line fed traffic to UP's main line at Cheyenne. General William Jackson Palmer, who oversaw construction of the western portions of KP, went on to build the narrow gauge Denver & Rio Grande (see chapter 3).

Kansas Pacific briefly competed with Union Pacific for traffic, but faced difficulties eking out an existence in the thinly populated plains of Kansas and eastern Colorado while relying upon UP for its westward connection. Jay Gould envisioned melding UP with KP in the mid-1870s, but that required a series of complex and controversial transactions. In 1880, Gould reorganized and combined UP, KP, and Denver Pacific, a move that nearly doubled UP's mileage by absorbing these potential competitors, which gave access to the vital Kansas City Gateway.

UP was drawn to tap the Colorado mining booms during the 1870s and 1880s. This initially resulted in a number of routes, many of them narrow gauge, built to reach Rocky Mountain mining camps. These efforts included leasing the mixed-gauge Colorado Central in 1879, which had extended a three-foot line from Golden to Central City, Colo., via mining camps at Georgetown, Colo., known for its famous Georgetown Loop. A year later, it acquired control of the three-foot-gauge Denver, South Park & Pacific, which served booming Leadville-area mines, and was aiming west toward the Gunnison, Colo., mining area. Later UP consolidated the DSP&P properties as its South Park Division. UP's Colorado-based expansion ended with its bankruptcy in 1893.

Northwest expansion

Union Pacific had eyed the Pacific Northwest as rich territory ripe for railroad transportation. Before construction of the transcontinental line to Promontory,

Utah Northern's 4-6-0 *Franklin* was an ornately decorated three-foot gauge locomotive that served the railroad in its earliest days. The railroad was converted to standard gauge in 1887 and absorbed by UP two years later.
Brian Solomon collection

CRÉDIT MOBILIER

Union Pacific's construction company, Crédit Mobilier of America, took its name from a French company—it was chosen to entice investors. In the 1860s it wasn't unusual for a railroad to pay its own construction firm for building a line, but under Thomas Durant, UP and Crédit Mobilier pushed this beyond the limits of acceptability. Crédit Mobilier earned a handsome return from the government by building UP. Essential to the organization were the brothers Oliver and Oakes Ames, both serving as directors. Oliver succeed John A. Dix as UP president during the crucial years of transcontinental construction, serving as acting president from 1866 to 1868 and as president from 1868 to 1871.

Years later, scandal erupted when the public learned that the company had maximized profits at taxpayer's expense often by grossly inflating cost estimates while too often doing less than an ideal job building the line. Even more egregious was that the owners of the Crédit Mobilier were largely the same people who controlled Union Pacific—several of whom held influential political positions and used gifts of Crédit Mobilier stock for personal and political gain. By 1873, the Crédit Mobilier had become one of the most publicized scandals of the 19th century, with the Ames brothers drawing great public anger. The scandal damaged Union Pacific's reputation for decades to come.

General Dodge surveyed routes to the Northwest. After the Golden Spike ceremony, the Northwest offered UP a direct outlet to the Pacific free from Central Pacific interests, while being able to serve lands rich with minerals, timber, and agricultural products. Portland was viewed as a gateway to Asia and a port that could allow UP to serve cities along the Pacific Coast via steamships. In 1879, UP finally expanded toward Oregon.

On the surface, the Oregon Short Line (OSL) appeared as an independent railroad, but it was effectively a UP line connecting with the mainline at Granger, Wyo. This route reached Shoshone, Idaho, in 1883,

Union Pacific in Utah
UP Union Pacific
HVR Heber Valley
SLGW Salt Lake, Garfield & Western
UC Utah Central
UTA Utah Transit Authority
UTAH Utah Railway
Other lines
DRGW Denver & Rio Grande Western
SP Southern Pacific
WP Western Pacific
© 2019, Kalmbach Media Co., TRAINS: Roen Kelly
Not all lines shown
0 10 20 30 40 50 miles
N
IDAHO
WYOMING
COLORADO
NEVADA
ARIZONA
UP to Pocatello, Idaho
Malad City
Preston
Cache Jct.
Logan
Bear Lake
Golden Spike completes first transcontinental railroad, May 10, 1869
Promontory
Bear River
Brigham City
Corrine
Promontory Point
Lucin
Montello
Hogup
Lakeside
OGDEN
Wasatch Mts.
Wahsatch
Evanston
Echo
UP to Cheyenne, Wyo.
UP to Sacramento, Calif.
Great Salt Lake Desert
GREAT SALT LAKE
Rowley
Wendover
Knolls
Delle
Burmester
Garfield
SALT LAKE CITY
Park City
Uinta Mountains
Bonneville Salt Flats
Cedar Mts.
Stansbury Mts.
Midvale
Copperton
Lehi
Heber City
Oquirrh Mts.
Gold Hill
Deep Creek Mts.
Utah Lake
PROVO
Springville
Spanish Fork
Lofgreen
Keigley
Thistle
Soldier Summit
Duchesne River
White River
Tintic
Colton
Castle Gate
Utah Rwy. Jct.
Helper
Clear Creek
Wildcat
Price
Nephi
Green River
Sunnyside
Tavaputs Plateau
Lynndyl
Sevier River
Mohrland
Mounds
Cedar
Delta
Woodside
Roan Cliffs
UP to Grand Junction and Denver, Colo.
Castle Valley
Book Cliffs
Grand Valley
Uncompahgre Plateau
Sevier Lake (dry)
Salina
Fillmore
Pahvant Mountains
Wasatch Plateau
San Rafael Swell
Green River
Solitude
Brendel
Thompson
Cisco
Black Rock
Green River Desert
Arches
Bootlegger Canyon
Potash
Milford
Marysvale
Escalante Desert
Lund
Iron Springs
Cedar City
Crestline
Iron Mountain
UP to Las Vegas, Nev.
Virgin River
UP (SP)
UP (WP)
(CP)
(UP)
UP (D&RGW)
(D&RGW)
UC
UTA
UP
HVR
UTAH

Union Pacific led the railroad industry in adopting efficient new technologies. In this 1954 publicity photo, UP agent J.L. Chance communicates with operators of mechanical icing machines via radio at a Pacific Fruit Express icing dock. *Union Pacific*

and extended a long branch north to the Wood River mining region in Idaho.

Henry Villard, a Portland-based financier, organized the Oregon Railway & Navigation Company (OR&N) in June 1879 to build eastward along the Columbia River toward the Idaho mining districts. Villard had previously served as the receiver for the Denver extension of the Kansas Pacific, and approached Gould to encourage UP to take part interest in the OR&N route, including a line over the Blue Mountains in eastern Oregon. In November 1884, OR&N reached Huntington, Ore., near the Idaho border—404 miles southeast of Portland—where it met the OSL. A last spike ceremony was staged on Nov. 25, 1884, but hardly anyone noticed. Regular passenger service began a week later. In the meantime Villard had taken control of Northern Pacific—one of UP's principal transcontinental rivals—which by 1883 had completed a connection with his OR&N near the confluence of the Columbia and Snake Rivers in eastern Oregon. However, funding NP's construction overextended Villard and he lost control of his empire.

Thus by 1887, UP controlled OR&N, which became an OSL subsidiary, and started extending branch lines across the Pacific Northwest that ultimately became important sources of freight traffic. UP consolidated its Pacific Northwest properties 1896, calling them the Oregon Railroad & Navigation Company, and then in 1910 changed the name to the Oregon-Washington Railway & Navigation Company.

During World War II, a woman operator at Fremont, Neb., hoops up train orders to the engineer on a Lima-built 2-10-2. UP was among many railroads during the war that broke with tradition by employing women in typically male-dominated crafts.
Union Pacific

The Harriman Era

UP finances weakened following Gould's death, and the Panic of 1893 sent the railroad into bankruptcy. This temporarily separated UP from its affiliated lines, including Denver Pacific, Kansas Pacific, and Oregon Short Line. By 1897, UP had been effectively pared down to its transcontinental trunk when financier E.H. Harriman, already involved with Illinois Central, saw the UP as an underutilized asset with enormous potential, suffering from mismanagement and poor finances. Harriman secured control in 1898, and thoroughly examined the railroad property. Unlike other financiers who left operations to subordinates, Harriman immersed himself in the details of UP's infrastructure, locomotives, and traffic. He learned about UP by speaking to its employees at length and listening to what they had to say. He then invested in UP to overcome its inadequacies.

A keen judge of men, Harriman worked with his top officers to find the best people to execute his ideas, while funding improvements that ultimately transformed Union Pacific from a weak player into one of the finest American railroads. However, the common myth that before Harriman the bankrupt UP was little more than "two streaks of rust across the plains" had little

For most of the 20th century, Chicago & North Western was UP's preferred interchange partner for forwarding freight and passenger traffic between Omaha and Chicago. In this undated World War II-era image, UP-C&NW and SP-UP-C&NW streamliners are lined up at Northwestern Terminal in Chicago. *Chicago & North Western*

truth to it. Historians note that in 1898 UP was a decent railroad and not a line limping along on a shoestring.

Harriman transformed the railroad into a transportation powerhouse. His detailed understanding of railroading earned the respect of his employees, fellow executives, and perhaps most importantly, the railroad's investors. Knowledge of railroading allowed him to materially improve UP's lines and increase its capability to haul goods and people. Harriman's biographer, George Kennan, summarized it thusly: "By reducing grades, eliminating curves, and increasing the size of cars and the tractive power of locomotives, he expected not only to lessen the road's operating expenses, but to double its carrying capacity."

Harriman wasted no time after taking control of UP to regain control of its affiliates, and soon he had Denver Pacific, Kansas Pacific, and OSL back on UP's map. His planned physical improvements initiated soon after he took control were ongoing

during his 11-year oversight and continued long after his untimely death in 1909. The main line between Omaha and Ogden benefited from numerous line relocations to correct the oversights of the original engineers and overcame limits of 1860s construction techniques. Improvements also involved upgrading bridges with new standardized steel structures of superior construction capable of carrying trains with higher axle loads and operating at faster speeds while lowering maintenance costs. Mainline tracks were upgraded with heavier rail and improved ballast, while capacity was increased by building directional double-track between Omaha and Ogden.

Harriman invested in state-of-the-art automatic block signaling (ABS) to prevent rear-end collisions and increase capacity. By 1909, more than 5,000 route-miles of Harriman's railroads were equipped with automatic block signals, which represented nearly 40% of all ABS installations in the U.S. The UP's standard lineside signals were Union Switch & Signal lower-quadrant semaphores, commonly using the Style B base-of-mast mechanism, and the lower quadrant semaphore was emblematic of Harriman safety.

Southern Pacific acquisition

Harriman viewed Central Pacific as a natural extension of the UP transcontinental route and shortly after taking control of UP, he approached C.P. Huntington, the last of the original "Big Four" directors, with an offer for the CP. Although the deal was refused, when Huntington died in 1900 Harriman was quick to take control of the entire Southern Pacific Co. (see chapter 3).

The Los Angeles & Salt Lake route

In the 1880s and 1890s, Union Pacific sent survey and construction teams to Nevada's remote Clover Creek Canyon and the Meadow Valley Wash as part of a formative scheme to reach Los Angeles; this effort stalled when UP's finances collapsed. At the turn of the 20th century, Senator W.A. Clark of Montana, the copper mogul, envisioned the future of Los Angeles and San Pedro as an international port and planned on building a new transcontinental railroad in competition with UP to develop the area. In 1901, Clark consolidated existing Los Angeles-area railroads while obtaining a charter for the San Pedro, Los

Sun Valley Stages operated a small fleet of Flxible buses to bring guests to Union Pacific's popular Sun Valley, Idaho resort. The buses were painted to match the railroad's famous streamliners. *Brian Solomon collection*

Harriman family members retained leadership roles at Union Pacific decades after E.H. Harriman's passing. UP Board chairman E. Roland Harriman and President A.E. Stoddard posed together on an inspection trip to Portland, Ore. *Union Pacific*

Freshly painted Spokane International Alco RS1 No. 1220 is at Lincoln, Neb., on June 5, 1962. The SI's RS1 fleet (Nos. 200-211) was renumbered by UP in 1962 as Nos. 1211-1222. Most were traded to Electro-Motive in 1969, while two later worked for Western Pacific affiliate Tidewater Southern. *Jim Seacrest*

Angeles & Salt Lake Railroad to connect its namesakes.

Harriman aimed to build along the same route, forcing cooperation with Clark. In 1902, Clark sold Harriman 50% of the SPLA&SL, placing the new line under UP's wing and supplying necessary financing to build from Salt Lake City via Las Vegas to southern California. Instead of building over the San Bernardino range to reach Los Angeles and the Pacific, SPLA&SL negotiated trackage rights on Santa Fe's line from Daggett to Barstow and over Cajon Pass to a junction near Riverside, Calif. From there UP built lines across L.A. Basin, reaching the port at San Pedro.

When Clark sold out to UP in the 1920s, San Pedro was dropped from the railroad's name (it had become part of Los Angeles in 1909) to become the Los Angeles & Salt Lake (LA&SL). This was UP's only direct route to California until it acquired Western Pacific in 1982. In the mid-1980s, Union Pacific developed the LA&SL as one of the first double-stack routes for land-bridge container traffic.

Harriman and Hill spark antitrust action

Harriman's nemesis was James J. Hill and his Great Northern transcontinental route. In the early 1900s, Hill and Harriman lines both improved their connections to Chicago. Great Northern's eastern terminus was in the Twin Cities, equivalent to UP's at Omaha, Neb./Council Bluffs, Iowa. From there, GN forwarded traffic via Chicago, Burlington & Quincy. Burlington's well-built network had lines from both the Twin Cities and Omaha to Chicago. Harriman had tried to secure Burlington as a friendly connection for UP east of Omaha, but Hill reacted by taking control of both Burlington and its owner, Northern Pacific. To accomplish this, Hill created a vast holding company called Northern Securities.

This effort appeared to be a giant consolidation of Great Northern, Northern Pacific, and Burlington into one all-powerful network. Harriman was unimpressed, and the public was alarmed at this new monopoly. To placate his naysayers, Hill offered the Harriman interests part

ownership in Northern Securities, which was one of the greatest political mistakes in early 20th-century business. The federal government was already alarmed over corporate monopolies, and the Hill-Harriman deal appeared to propose a total transportation monopoly involving both railroad systems. The tidal wave of public outrage which followed spurred government action against the railroads.

Northern Securities was a prime focus of President Theodore Roosevelt's crusade against American big business. The U.S. Supreme Court ruled against Northern Securities in 1904, initiating a series of high-profile antitrust actions that over the next decade had disastrous consequences for the entire railroad industry. It signaled the end of many American railroad affiliations, including Harriman's UP-Southern Pacific combination, while making it difficult for railroads to raise capital for route expansion or improvements.

World War, Depression, and post-war prosperity

During the lead-up to American involvement in World War I, the American railroad network as a whole had begun to bog down from a swell of traffic. The situation became untenable, and by the end of 1917 the federal government stepped in to take control of railroad operations. For approximately two years, the United States Railroad Administration (USRA) operated the majority of American railroads.

During the mid-20th century the UP focused on traffic development rather than route expansion. The UP (and other railroads) regained control of their properties in March 1920, and while freight traffic grew through the decade, passenger business suffered as result of increased public spending on highways and the growth of the automotive industry. The onset of the Great Depression in the 1930s devastated railroad traffic, which only began to recover toward the end of the decade. World War II set new records for traffic carried on most American railroads and accelerated development of West Coast ports, which greatly aided UP.

America's westward focus throughout the mid-1900s resulted in healthy growth among Western railroads despite lines in the East struggling from intense highway competition, short hauls, and industrial decline. UP also benefited from development of the vast natural resources along the land-grant properties it acquired during its construction.

An Electro-Motive switcher works at a yard circa 1950, possibly in Los Angeles. The scene is dominated by the 40- and 50-foot boxcars of the era; some passenger cars and a string of ice-bunker refrigerator cars in ventilator service occupy tracks behind the switcher.
Trains collection

Spokane International

In the late 1950s, when the American railroad merger movement was heating up, UP acquired Spokane International, a minor transaction often neglected in the bigger story of railroad consolidation. The 152-mile SI connected with UP at Spokane, Wash., and ran north to Eastport, Idaho, on the Canadian border where it interchanged freight with Canadian Pacific. It had a nine-mile branch that reached Coeur d'Alene, Idaho. The railroad began operations in 1906, and when UP took control, the railroad had 12 Alco RS1 locomotives and approximately 200 freight cars. UP dressed the Alcos in its corporate paint scheme and has continued to operate SI ever since.

Sad story of the Rock Island Lines

The Chicago, Rock Island & Pacific was formed in the mid-19th century by consolidating smaller lines, and adopted its name in 1866. Commonly known as the Rock Island Lines, the railroad expanded rapidly across the Midwest from the late 1800s through early 1900s, encompassing a network of lines connecting the gateways of Chicago, Colorado Springs, Colo., Dallas, Denver, Kansas City, Memphis, Tenn., Omaha, Neb., Peoria, Ill., St. Louis, and

A model of a Union Pacific two-section "super turbine" attracts considerable enthusiasm in this 1950s publicity photo. UP's request for the last order of gas-turbine locomotives from GE was for a locomotive capable of delivering 7,000 hp at an altitude of 7,000 feet. When delivered they were rated at 8,500 hp and numbered 1-30. *Union Pacific*

Tucumcari, N.M., with routes extending to South Dakota and Louisiana. In the late 1940s, Rock Island operated 7,649 miles (including approximately 480 miles of trackage rights). The railroad was a "granger line" that depended on the movement of agricultural products, but just about everywhere it went it faced stiff competition from other railroads with better finances and superior routes. The struggling line was bankrupt from 1914 to 1917 and again between 1933 and 1948.

Rock Island opened merger talks with Union Pacific in 1963, and a petition to merge the two went to the Interstate Commerce Commission (ICC). Unfortunately, the ICC took more than 10 years to ponder the UP-Rock Island combination; in that time Rock Island went to seed, deferring maintenance on most routes. At the end of 1974, the ICC finally approved the merger but with a variety of onerous conditions to appease railroads that had objected to the merger. By that point the Rock Island had fallen into such a poor physical and financial state that the UP decided it was no longer interested, and pulled out of the merger. In March 1975, the Rock Island declared bankruptcy for the third time; it would not recover.

The Rock Island struggled on for a few more years, but on March 31, 1980 it was liquidated, with its locomotives and rolling stock sold and its most-attractive routes parceled out to other carriers. Significantly, Chicago & North Western bought the Twin Cities-Kansas City "Spine Line"; Southern Pacific (through subsidiary St. Louis Southwestern) bought the Kansas City-Tucumcari route; and Missouri-Kansas-Texas formed its Oklahoma-Kansas-Texas subsidiary to serve shippers on portions of the Rock Island in those states. This new railroad handled wheat and corn from Kansas and Oklahoma, and aggregate and sand products from Texas.

All three of these disconnected Rock Island routes were ultimately integrated in UP's expanded system as result of mergers with C&NW, SP and M-K-T. Other significant portions of the Rock Island were sold to short lines or regional carriers, with some of the weakest routes abandoned altogether. Unfortunately, Rock Island's Tucumcari-Memphis route was abandoned. This line had no direct parallel and would have a made an ideal direct route for intermodal traffic moving from southern California to the Memphis gateway.

Merger mania

Union Pacific recognized that railroading in the entire West was ripe for consolidation following the Burlington Northern merger of 1970, which finally sewed together James J. Hill's historic rail empire by combining the Burlington, Great Northern, Northern Pacific, and Spokane, Portland & Seattle into one system. Maury Klein in his *Union Pacific—The Reconfiguration,* a book dedicated to former UP President and Chairman John C. Kenefick, explains that

This 1960s rendering of twin-engined Centennial diesel No. 6900 depicts the locomotive working a freight in the rugged desert scenery along the Los Angeles & Salt Lake Route. The DDA40Xs were numbered in the 6900s to commemorate the 100th anniversary of the Golden Spike. *Union Pacific*

under Kenefick in the 1970s UP initiated an intensive investigation to remain competitive and find the most suitable candidates for merger by carefully analyzing a host of considerations including route structure, finances, traffic, and corporate cultures.

After the proposed Rock Island merger fizzled, UP considered merger with C&NW, which in the mid-1970s was handling almost 60% of UP's traffic between Omaha and Chicago and was deemed to have the best routes between these two key gateways. Not only did UP-C&NW interchange at Omaha-Council Bluffs, but also via a cutoff between Fremont, Neb., and Missouri Valley, Iowa, a route that was shorter and less congested than other routes. Traffic notwithstanding, UP held off acquiring C&NW in the 1970s because of the railroad's poor financial condition. This was prior to C&NW's expansion into Wyoming's Powder River Basin in the early 1980s, which increased cooperation between the two railroads and improved C&NW's traffic and finances.

UP deemed Western Pacific another logical acquisition. The UP-SP's historic Ogden interchange arrangements with SP had been canceled back in 1968; since that time SP had gradually routed less traffic via Ogden, instead sending its business east via its Sunset and Golden State routes. This gave SP a longer haul, which didn't benefit UP. The WP was a minor player that couldn't compete effectively against the gigantic SP. It only operated a handful of freights daily in each direction between Salt Lake City and California. By the late 1970s, WP was looking for a merger partner and UP didn't want WP to fall into the hands of a competitor.

In the meantime, UP identified the Missouri Pacific as another ideal candidate, in part because of its robust chemical traffic with access to the Memphis and St. Louis gateways and Gulf Coast ports. Traffic across MP's territory was strong and growing, and UP's top management was very impressed by MP's operations and management team. When Burlington Northern announced it was acquiring the St. Louis-San Francisco (Frisco), which served much of same territory as MP, UP must have felt compelled to make a move.

Parallel with UP's search for merger partners was federal deregulation of transportation, culminating with the Staggers Act of 1980. This lifted many of the rate and traffic restrictions that had hemmed in railroads through much of the

Missouri Pacific SD40 No. 3002 leads a southbound freight on the morning of Aug. 16, 1980, alongside Highway 90 near Delaplaine, Ark. Built in 1967, the locomotive was originally MP No. 702. In 1984 it was became No. 4002 and painted in UP colors; it was retired in 1989. *Scott Muskopf*

20th century, and also relaxed government oversight, but encouraged all transportation modes to seek means to remain competitive. This revolutionary regulatory transformation spurred a host of mergers over the next decade and a half.

In 1980, Union Pacific surprised observers by initiating simultaneous acquisitions of both MP and WP. Its timing was in part a reaction to the BN-SLSF merger, and in part to the new deregulated environment stimulated by Staggers. The UP-MP-WP merger, commonly referred to as the "Mop-Up," was approved by the ICC in 1982, and the railroads were merged in December of that year. Western Pacific provided UP with its own direct route into northern California, initially operated as UP's Fourth Division. This enabled UP to shift the majority of its Overland traffic away from the Ogden interchange. Missouri Pacific was a 3,130-mile network connecting with Union Pacific at several locations, notably Omaha and Kansas City, providing Union Pacific access to a host of new markets in Kansas, Missouri, Illinois, Oklahoma, Arkansas, Louisiana, and Texas. MP initially retained its corporate identity and a degree of independence; it was finally legally absorbed into UP on March 1, 1997.

In May 1988, UP acquired the Missouri-Kansas-Texas—the Katy—and assigned it to its Missouri Pacific subsidiary. By the end of the year, Katy's operations had been melded with MP's.

In 1989, Union Pacific purchased a 25% interest in its longtime eastern interchange partner, Chicago & North Western. Then in the summer 1994, when BN and Santa Fe surprised the industry with their unpredicted merger proposal, UP responded with a controversial counteroffer for Santa Fe. That offer was soon rebuffed, but drove up the price BN had to pay for Santa Fe. Ultimately BNSF was approved by the ICC, beginning operations in September 1995. In the meantime, UP merged with C&NW, primarily seeking to secure its Overland Route connection to Chicago as well as C&NW's Powder River coal access.

The sprawling North Platte, Neb., hump yard was a $3.5 million project at the time of this photo in 1948. This view is from the top of the hump looking toward the bowl tracks. *Union Pacific*

On the morning of Nov. 11, 2003, Dash-9 No. 9744 leads an eastbound manifest freight in the Feather River Canyon near Keddie, Calif. Following clearance and capacity improvements to its former SP Donner Pass crossing during 2008-2010, UP diverted most through freight away from the former WP route in favor of Donner Pass. *Brian Solomon*

The merger with C&NW hadn't yet settled down when in September 1995 Union Pacific announced that it intended to acquire Southern Pacific (including the former Rio Grande and Cotton Belt). This enormously controversial merger proposal spurred a complex debate regarding railroad competition in the West. Sensing opportunity or the threat to existing order, various railroads asked to extend their reach by acquiring portions of UP or SP, or obtaining trackage rights over UP to provide competition. One of the most interesting proposals came from Conrail's bid for SP's Cotton Belt routes, on the premise that an unchecked UP-SP combination would have a near monopoly in the petrochemical markets of Louisiana and Texas, and so Conrail could offer necessary competition. UP dismissed this proposal and others. Rather than negotiate with myriad railroads, UP focused on BNSF and offered its primary competitor broad trackage rights along with some strategic lines to appease important customers and address competitive concerns.

As UP's undertaking was unfolding, the ICC itself was disbanded and its regulatory and merger-deciding function allocated to the newly created Surface Transportation

Passing beneath the former Chicago & North Western coaling tower in Clyman, Wis., SD70ACe No. 8862 leads business train PNABU2 10 toward Milwaukee on Sept. 10, 2014. The wide supports on the coaling tower date from a time when C&NW's Adams Line was a busy double-track route. *Chris Guss*

Board (STB). The STB approved UP-SP with BNSF and Kansas City Southern trackage-rights provisions in July 1996. The merger went into effect on Sept. 11, 1996. So, 84 years after they were separated, Harriman's western railroads were again joined as one unified company.

The first year of integration with SP proved rougher than expected. Merging two enormous railroad networks with differing corporate cultures was far more complicated than anyone realized. Ultimately, UP made massive investments to improve former SP routes, including adding track to the heavily traveled Sunset Route (Los Angeles-New Orleans) and improving overhead clearances on SP's Donner Pass crossing.

UP made a variety of changes to the way it moved trains. In August 1997, it stopped operating the former Rio Grande route over Tennessee Pass. Part of UP's revised freight strategy resulted in the closing of the former Missouri Pacific line to Pueblo, Colo., which connected with the Tennessee Pass route. In July 1998, UP offered to sell a 12-mile section of the line through the Royal Gorge to a Cañon City, Colorado-based tourist line called the Royal Gorge Express that has been running the line as the Royal Gorge Route. Also in 1998, UP and BNSF announced the

Union Pacific SD70M No. 4332 was repainted in a special scheme in the spring of 2021 to celebrate the company's numerous employee resource groups. The road number was changed to 1979 to reflect the year UP's first resource group was established. The locomotive was displayed on Aug. 3, 2021 at Proviso yard near Chicago. *Chris Guss*

sale of their jointly owned Camus Prairie Railroad in Idaho to shortline operator North American RailNet. Two years later, operations on portions of that railroad were curtailed and tracks later removed over much of the route.

In 2012, UP marked the 150th anniversary of the signing of the Pacific Railroad Act with system-wide steam excursions led by popular Heritage Fleet steam locomotive No. 844 covering more

The biggest locomotive on the anniversary of the big day! Big Boy No. 4014 couples to its consist at Ogden Station during the 150th anniversary of the Golden Spike on May 10, 2019. Completion of the transcontinental railroad in 1869 was one of the great moments of 19th century America. *Bob Karambelas*

than 13,000 miles. The railroad continued to honor its locomotive heritage in 2013 when it reacquired Big Boy steam locomotive No. 4014 from the Southern California chapter of the Railway & Locomotive Historical Society. The UP moved moved No. 4014 from Pomona, Calif., where it had been on static display, to Cheyenne for an operational restoration. The locomotive made its cross-country move by rail in Spring 2014, and over the next five years was completely restored by a team led by Ed Dickens, UP's Heritage Fleet operations director. Among the changes to the locomotive was converting it from coal- to oil-fired. Nearly six decades after the Big Boy fleet exited revenue service, No. 4014 made its first public trips in 2019 to mark the 150th anniversary of the Golden Spike ceremony at Promontory, Utah. It has since traveled around the system entertaining thousands of onlookers.

Union Pacific business train PALG3 03 rolls south on the Milwaukee Subdivision at Bain, Wis., on June 3, 2020. SD70ACe No. 1111 was repainted in June 2019 to honor the men and women of the railroad. *Chris Guss*

As of 2021, Union Pacific Railroad is the operating company of the Union Pacific Corporation. Lance Fritz serves as Chairman, President, and Chief Executive Officer. UP boasts that its system spans 32,452 route-miles, serves an estimated 10,000 customers in 23 states, and rosters 7,476 locomotives. The railroad employs nearly one person for every route mile.

CHAPTER 2

PREDECESSOR HISTORIES

Union Pacific added to its system many times through mergers and other acquisitions, including several lines that were major railroads of their eras

On July 13, 1998, locomotives of predecessor railroads are working on UP at Muncie, Kan. Chicago & North Western AC4400CW No. 8830 leads westbound coal empties toward West Elk Mine in Colorado, while Southern Pacific AC4400CW No. 251 is working as a DPU on the rear of a loaded Powder River coal train to San Antonio, Texas. The Marysville Subdivision west of Kansas City has served as a coal conduit for decades, hosting trains for power plants in the Midwest and South. *Chris Guss*

251
251
251
Southern Pacific
SP

Predecessor railroads that became part of Union Pacific each had unique histories and stories of how they developed and grew. Many were themselves formed through mergers and by purchasing smaller lines.

Chicago & North Western (former Minneapolis & St. Louis) Alco RS1 No. 227 has just left the Railway Transfer Yard on its old home rails in the Minneapolis milling district. At left is the Washburn "A" Mill—now the Mill City Museum. *Joe Elliott, Aaron Isaacs collection*

Chicago & North Western

Chicago & North Western Railway, which grew to be one of the largest transportation systems west of Chicago, was the product of the reorganization of the ill-financed Chicago, St. Paul & Fond du Lac Rail Road in 1859. C&NW was true to its name and built north and west from its headquarters city, Chicago, reaching across the upper Midwest and Great Plains. It absorbed a host of smaller railroads, including the pioneering Galena & Chicago Union Railroad, which in 1848 had been the first line to build westward from Chicago. Among the many components eventually melded into the C&NW system was the Chicago, St. Paul, Minneapolis & Omaha Railway, known as the "The Omaha Road," which ran from Omaha northwest to Minneapolis-St. Paul and Duluth, Minn. Through the steam era this line had retained some independence under the wing of C&NW.

The North Western was unusual for its left-hand running on directional double-track lines, which made for some interesting platform arrangements at Chicago suburban passenger stations, and potentially complicated interfaces with other double-track railroads. It was among early proponents of automatic block signals and was among a few Midwestern lines that adopted Hall disc signals (often descriptively called "banjo signals") on some routes.

Later, it worked with General Railway Signal to create a unique short-blade style of semaphore that became standard across its system. In the color-light-signal era, it developed the distinctive practice of multiple-light signal heads set horizontally rather the vertically.

Among C&NW's most famous passenger trains were its *400s,* so named for the length in miles of its Chicago-Twin Cities run. This led to C&NW's crack collection of 1930s and later passenger trains to be collectively named "The *400* Fleet." In the 1950s the railroad was a pioneer in adopting bi-level "gallery style" push-pull suburban passenger equipment.

The C&NW faced competition from other regional lines, since its network overlapped with portions of the Burlington, Milwaukee Road, Rock Island, and Soo Line. While considered a "granger" line—with lots of agricultural traffic—its routes and traffic were varied widely, from iron ore traffic in Michigan's Upper Peninsula to coal from central Illinois and lonely,

Chicago Great Western was among the railroads acquired by Chicago & North Western in the mid-1900s. In 1966, two years before the merger, a pair of CGW GP30s lead a freight through Westminster Junction on Great Northern's line in St. Paul, Minn. A Northern Pacific caboose hop is westbound on NP's line.
Aaron Issacs

high-plains grain-hauling lines in South Dakota and Wyoming. In later years, C&NW's most important route was its Chicago-Omaha main line. Of the six main lines in this important corridor, C&NW was Union Pacific's preferred route for its transcontinental traffic heading to and from Chicago.

The railroad's largest yard was its sprawling Proviso installation west of downtown Chicago. Also important were yards at Marshalltown, Iowa. After World War II, the C&NW system consisted of 9,539 route miles across Illinois, Iowa, Michigan, Minnesota, Missouri, Nebraska, North Dakota, South Dakota, Wisconsin, and Wyoming.

The C&NW was very active in the mid-20th century merger movement. Ben Heineman had come to the railroad from Minneapolis & St. Louis, a marginal but well-run line that connected the Twin Cities with Peoria, Ill., an important as a western gateway that avoided the congestion of Chicago. Heineman oversaw a series of mergers aimed at securing greater traffic for C&NW while eliminating competition. In 1958, C&NW absorbed the Litchfield & Madison to gain access to St. Louis. Next was Heineman's Minneapolis & St. Louis, merged into C&NW in 1960. The largest addition was the 1,411-mile Chicago Great Western, a cross-shaped system centered on Oelwein, Iowa, that connected Chicago with Omaha and the Twin Cities with Kansas City (via Des Moines). Although controversial, the ICC approved this merger in 1967; C&NW absorbed the line a year later.

From the late 1960s until its merger with UP in 1995, C&NW gradually pared back its trackage (especially its vast network

On April 22, 1995, shortly before merging with UP, fresh C&NW Dash 9-44CWs lead Powder River coal empties westward near Maple River, Iowa, on the Chicago-Council Bluffs main line.
Brian Solomon

of low-traffic branch lines) to its most sustainable core, yet continued to make strategic acquisitions and extensions where it was beneficial. In 1980, when Rock Island was liquidated, C&NW bought its Twin Cities-Kansas City "Spine Line." Four years later, C&NW expanded into Wyoming's Power River Basin coal fields with help from Union Pacific.

By the mid-1980s, there was very little left of routes of either M&StL or CGW, and many of C&NW's own original routes had been truncated or consolidated. Rather than maintain long sections of lightly used secondary lines simply to forward traffic, C&NW had worked out arrangements with parallel carriers that enabled abandoning all but its most profitable trackage, leaving it with a variety of disconnected "island" operations isolated from the rest of its network.

In its final years, C&NW was largely focused on forwarding UP's east-west traffic between Fremont/Omaha and Chicago and handling coal traffic from the Powder River.

Union Pacific acquired C&NW in spring 1995, purchasing the 70% of C&NW that it did not already own.

Denver & Rio Grande Western

Union Pacific didn't acquire Denver & Rio Grande Western directly, but got the line's trackage when it merged with SP in 1996. This erstwhile long-time competitor to UP, whose slogan once boasted "Through the Rockies, not around them," had a long, colorful history, but its route only serves as a relatively minor component of the modern UP network.

The Rio Grande's history traces to 1870 with General William Jackson Palmer's vision for a narrow gauge line called Denver

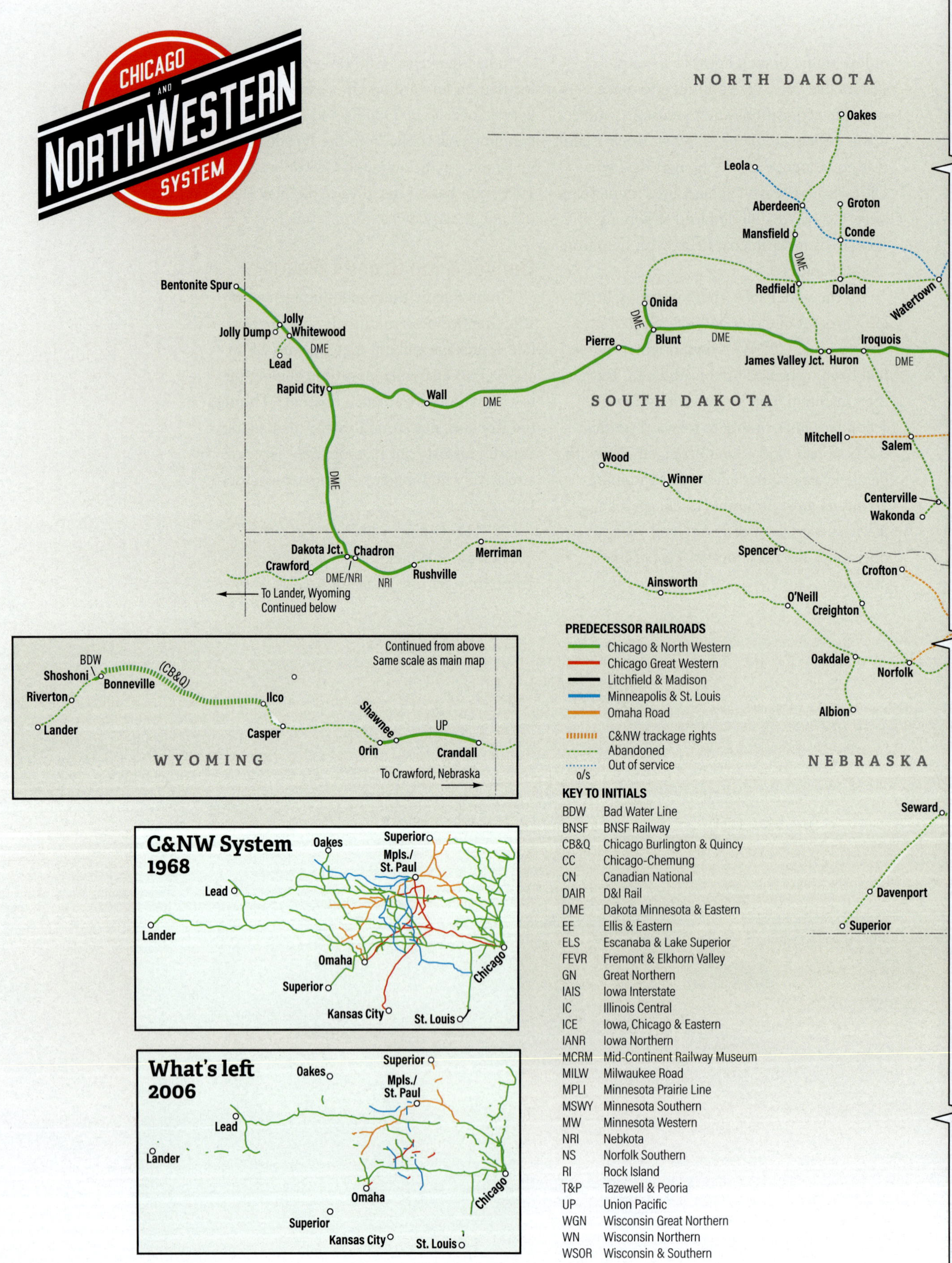
CHICAGO AND NORTHWESTERN SYSTEM
NORTH DAKOTA
SOUTH DAKOTA
NEBRASKA
WYOMING
Oakes
Leola
Aberdeen
Groton
Mansfield
Conde
Redfield
Doland
Watertown
Onida
Pierre
Blunt
James Valley Jct.
Huron
Iroquois
Bentonite Spur
Jolly
Jolly Dump
Whitewood
Lead
Rapid City
Wall
DME
Mitchell
Salem
Wood
Winner
Centerville
Wakonda
Dakota Jct.
Chadron
Crawford
DME/NRI
NRI
Rushville
Merriman
Spencer
Crofton
Ainsworth
O'Neill
Creighton
To Lander, Wyoming
Continued below
Oakdale
Norfolk
Albion
Continued from above
Same scale as main map
BDW
Shoshoni
Bonneville
(CB&Q)
Riverton
Lander
Ilco
Casper
Shawnee
UP
Orin
Crandall
To Crawford, Nebraska
PREDECESSOR RAILROADS
Chicago & North Western
Chicago Great Western
Litchfield & Madison
Minneapolis & St. Louis
Omaha Road
C&NW trackage rights
Abandoned
Out of service
o/s
KEY TO INITIALS
BDW Bad Water Line
BNSF BNSF Railway
CB&Q Chicago Burlington & Quincy
CC Chicago-Chemung
CN Canadian National
DAIR D&I Rail
DME Dakota Minnesota & Eastern
EE Ellis & Eastern
ELS Escanaba & Lake Superior
FEVR Fremont & Elkhorn Valley
GN Great Northern
IAIS Iowa Interstate
IC Illinois Central
ICE Iowa, Chicago & Eastern
IANR Iowa Northern
MCRM Mid-Continent Railway Museum
MILW Milwaukee Road
MPLI Minnesota Prairie Line
MSWY Minnesota Southern
MW Minnesota Western
NRI Nebkota
NS Norfolk Southern
RI Rock Island
T&P Tazewell & Peoria
UP Union Pacific
WGN Wisconsin Great Northern
WN Wisconsin Northern
WSOR Wisconsin & Southern
Seward
Davenport
Superior
C&NW System 1968
Oakes
Superior
Mpls./St. Paul
Lead
Lander
Omaha
Chicago
Superior
Kansas City
St. Louis
What's left 2006
Superior
Oakes
Mpls./St. Paul
Lead
Lander
Omaha
Chicago
Superior
Kansas City
St. Louis

© 2006 Kalmbach Publishing Co., TRAINS: Bill Metzger

Rio Grande continued to operate portions of its three-foot gauge network into the mid-20th century. On Aug. 15, 1952, a Baldwin 2-8-2 Mikado works as a helper ahead of the caboose on a Monarch Branch freight at the Garfield Wye in Colorado. The D&RGW converted profitable sections of this line to standard gauge in 1956. *John E. Pickett*

In 1930, Alco built 10 simple (single-expansion) 2-8-8-2s for Rio Grande. These imposing, powerful steam locomotives were well suited to the railroad's mountainous mainline operations. In 1953, Rio Grande No. 3613 poses for a photo at the roundhouse in Grand Junction, Colo. *Robert A. Buck*

& Rio Grande, which was originally projected to connect Denver with Mexico City. The first section opened in October 1871 from Denver to Lake Divide, Colo. The railroad faced insurmountable hurdles in its goal to cross the Rio Grande and reach Mexico, so changed direction in the late 1870s. It then faced off with the Santa Fe, which was building west through the same territory. The two lines fought—literally, with guns—for control of key western routes. A truce was reached: D&RG gave up on pushing toward Mexico and shifted its focus west towards the developing Colorado mining districts and Salt Lake City.

Rio Grande built over Le Veta Pass, reaching Alamosa, Colo., by 1878, and continued west via its San Juan extension over Cumbres Pass to Chama, N.M., and beyond to Durango, Colo., with a branch north to Silverton, Colo., and south from Antonito to Santa Fe, N.M. It also built a route through the narrow confines of the Royal Gorge—which had been the source of great friction between it and Santa Fe, and in its early days resulted in dual-gauge track shared with Santa Fe. This route allowed Rio Grande to reach the productive Leadville mining district in 1881, and was ultimately part of a line extended over Tennessee Pass that was later standard-gauged to become a main line to the West. Another route reached westward from a connection with the Royal Gorge route at Salida, Colo., crossing Marshall Pass and going through Black Canyon along the Gunnison River to reach Grand Junction, Colo. By 1883, Rio Grande's narrow gauge affiliate Denver & Rio Grande Western had connected to Salt Lake City. The two similarly named companies suffered from periods of animosity and cooperation in their

The late-era Rio Grande operated a compact Rocky Mountain network in Colorado and Utah. Here GP40 No. 3082 descends from Soldier Summit near Kyune, Utah, in September 1989.
Brian Solomon

operation of a through route between Denver and Salt Lake City—which was converted to standard gauge by 1890—but the two lines did not formally merge until 1908.

Jay Gould added Rio Grande to his portfolio of railroads in the early 1880s, and although he sold most of his interest in the railroad before his death in 1890, a decade later his son re-acquired control and made it a key component for his transcontinental scheme along with Missouri Pacific. Gould lost control in 1920, although Rio Grande continued to maintain a significant interchange with MP at Pueblo. The railroad was reorganized in 1924 as the Denver & Rio Grande Western Railroad.

The advantages of building narrow gauge lines—mainly cheaper construction and less-expensive, smaller equipment—gradually took a back seat to the realities of interchange with other railroads. Rio Grande began converting primary routes to standard

This early 1950s advertisement for Missouri-Kansas-Texas freight service featured an artistic rendition of the railroad's Electro-Motive F3s. *Brian Solomon collection*

After World War II, Missouri-Kansas-Texas placed several orders for Alco-GE road diesels. In 1952, two FA freight units lead a southbound train at the Hattie Street viaduct out of Fort Worth, Texas. In the late 1950s, M-K-T had many of its FAs repowered with EMD 16-567 diesel engines. *Trains collection*

gauge and abandoning lines with little traffic, although portions of its narrow gauge system survived for the next 75 years. The last vestiges of the Rio Grande common-carrier narrow gauge network survived until the late 1960s, and were among the last steam-hauled common-carrier lines in the United States. Two portions today survive as tourist railways: Durango & Silverton between its namesake cities through the scenic Animus Canyon, and the Cumbres & Toltec Scenic over Cumbres Pass between Antonito, Colo., and Chama, N.M.

In the early 20th century, railroad visionary David Moffat set about building a competing transcontinental link west from Denver through the Colorado Front Range. The railroad was initially called Denver,

On Feb. 15, 1981, Katy northbound freight No. 102 is at Pitman Hill Road south of St. Charles, Mo., on the lightly used St. Louis Subdivision. The crew was short on time while the train is still 26 miles short of Katy's Baden Yard in St. Louis.
Scott Muskopf

Northwestern & Pacific, but after Moffat died in 1911 the railroad was renamed the Denver & Salt Lake and embarked on landmark improvements. The most impressive was the 32,799-foot Moffat tunnel that crossed below the Continental Divide. The tunnel was completed in 1928, allowing the railroad to abandon its sinuous high-altitude crossing over Rollins Pass, which crested at 11,660 feet. Despite the long tunnel, the D&SL route was a dead-end line until 1934, when the Dotsero Cutoff was completed to form a through connection to Rio Grande's main line, finally enabling D&SL to connect its namesake cities. D&SL and Rio Grande were formally merged in 1947. In the 1950s and 1960s, Rio Grande's standard gauge

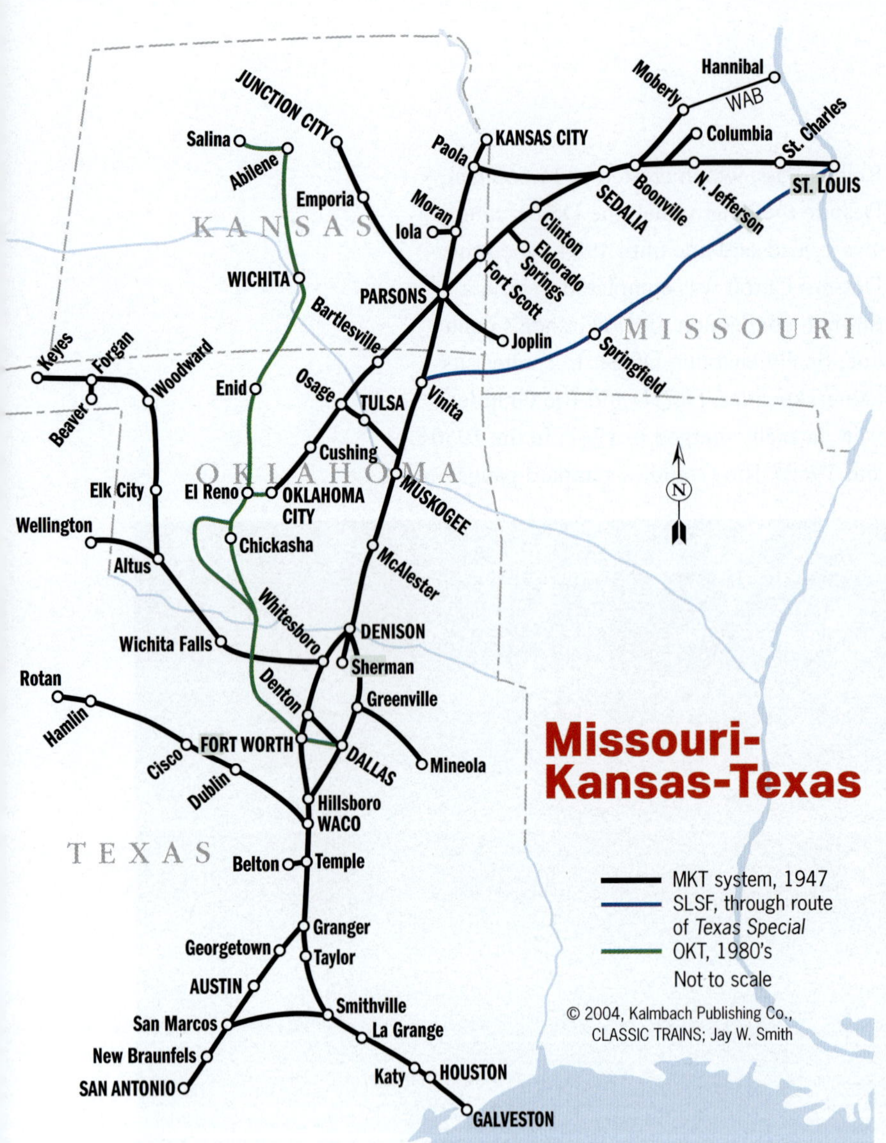

lines hosted robust traffic. High-yield, low-sulfur coal on the west end of the old D&SL and in Utah kept the lines west of the tunnel busy over the years.

The advent of the Staggers Act in 1980 had profound implications for Rio Grande. The MP-WP-UP merger cut off friendly connections at both ends of its main line, which threatened the volume of through traffic. In 1984, Denver-based Anschutz Corporation acquired the Rio Grande. The ICC's unfavorable ruling regarding the Santa Fe-Southern Pacific merger enabled Anschutz to acquire SP in 1988, placing the two railroads under common ownership. (Although it was D&RGW that purchased SP, it was the SP name and paint scheme that was used for the railroad and equipment after that point.)

Over the next few years SP gradually dominated, while flooding Rio Grande's main lines with through traffic. The SP utilized Rio Grande trackage rights over Missouri Pacific (awarded in 1981 with the UP-MP merger) to reach Kansas City and ultimately Chicago. This corridor was busy with freights until the 1996 UP-SP merger.

In April 1983, M-K-T RS3M No. 143 backs past the yard office at Bellmead, Texas. It is one of 15 Alco RS3s sent to EMD to be re-engined in 1959 and emerged with an EMD GP-style rear hood. Six were still working at the UP merger; they were retired shortly after UP took over. *Lewis Raby, Tom Kline collection*

Thundering past the derelict Rock Island depot at Kingfisher, Okla., M-K-T GP40 No. 221 leads unit grain train 603 toward Fort Worth, Texas, shortly after Katy's Oklahoma-Kansas-Texas subsidiary began operations on portions of the former Rock Island. This was a cooperative venture formed to serve shippers after the demise of the Rock Island on March 31, 1980, and these lines remain part of UP's system. *Tom Kline*

BNSF gained trackage rights via the Moffat Tunnel route between Denver and Salt Lake City, but in 1997 UP closed Rio Grande's steep-grade main line over Tennessee Pass in favor of routing traffic over the Moffat route, abandoned portions of its Missouri Pacific line east of Pueblo, and diverted most through traffic to its transcon route across Wyoming. The Moffat route has continued serve coal traffic and also hosts Amtrak's *California Zephyr* and BNSF freights. (See the map on page 62).

Missouri-Kansas-Texas

To the novice historian, the Missouri-Kansas-Texas may seem to have been a logical predecessor to Union Pacific. The line originated in 1865 with a company confusingly called Union Pacific South Branch, which had no corporate ties to the transcontinental Union Pacific. Its only early physical connection to UP was at Junction City, Kan., a virtually unknown crossroads. In 1870, the Missouri, Kansas & Texas Railway was formed from the UPSB. It became known as the "Katy" from the common pronunciation of its reporting marks.

The line was bought by Jay Gould, who controlled it between 1873 to 1888 and incorporated it into his expanding Missouri Pacific empire. Under his direction the M-K-T enjoyed solid management and modest growth. Gould gave up the line during an economic panic, but the railroad recovered in 1891 and continued to prosper through the early 1900s. It was the first railroad constructed in what became the state of Oklahoma. Katy reached the Texas border by 1872, Dallas in 1886, Houston in 1893, and finally San Antonio a few years later. Pushing northward, M-K-T tapped the St. Louis gateway in the 1880s while making an important connection to Kansas City in 1904. By 1915, the railroad spanned nearly 4,000 miles.

Katy's traffic and finances suffered from rapid expansion and meandering routes that overlapped with competing railroads,

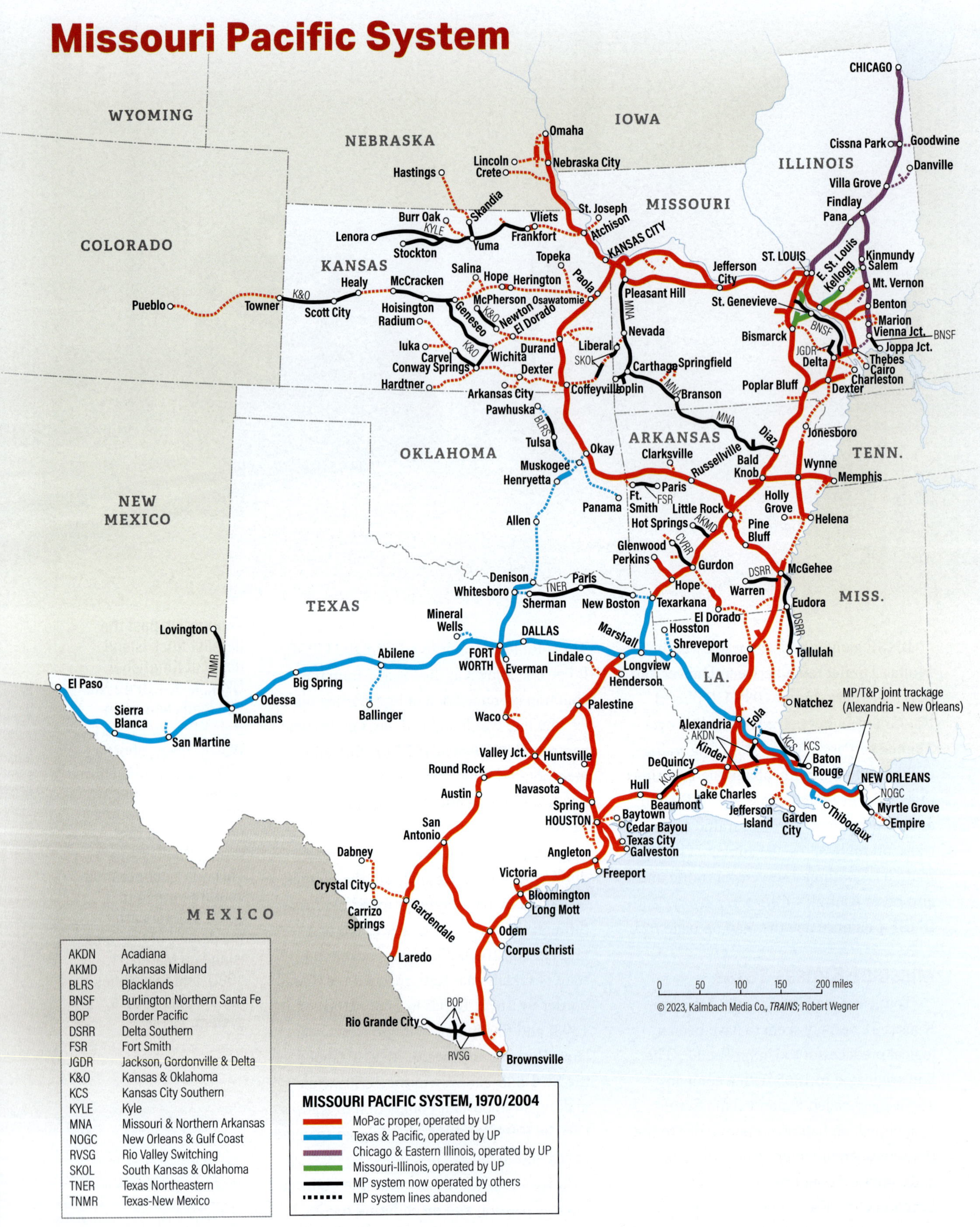

Missouri Pacific System
WYOMING
NEBRASKA
IOWA
ILLINOIS
MISSOURI
COLORADO
KANSAS
OKLAHOMA
ARKANSAS
TENN.
NEW MEXICO
TEXAS
LA.
MISS.
MEXICO
CHICAGO
Cissna Park
Goodwine
Danville
Villa Grove
Findlay
Pana
Kinmundy
Salem
Mt. Vernon
Benton
Marion
Vienna Jct.
BNSF
Joppa Jct.
Thebes
Cairo
Charleston
Dexter
E. St. Louis
Kellogg
ST. LOUIS
Jefferson City
St. Genevieve
Bismarck
BNSF
JGDR
Delta
Poplar Bluff
Jonesboro
Omaha
Lincoln
Crete
Nebraska City
Hastings
Burr Oak
KYLE
Skandia
Vliets
Frankfort
St. Joseph
Atchison
KANSAS CITY
Lenora
Stockton
Yuma
Topeka
Salina
Hope
Herington
Paola
Pleasant Hill
MNA
Nevada
Pueblo
Towner
K&O
Scott City
Healy
McCracken
Hoisington
Radium
McPherson
K&O
Newton
Osawatomie
El Dorado
Geneseo
K&O
Iuka
Carvel
Conway Springs
Wichita
Durand
Dexter
Hardtner
Arkansas City
Liberal
SKOL
Coffeyville
Joplin
Carthage
Springfield
MNA
Branson
MNA
Diaz
Pawhuska
BLRS
Tulsa
Okay
Muskogee
Henryetta
Clarksville
Russellville
Bald Knob
Wynne
Memphis
Paris
FSR
Ft. Smith
Panama
Little Rock
Holly Grove
Helena
Allen
Hot Springs
AKMD
Pine Bluff
Glenwood
CVRR
Perkins
Gurdon
DSRR
McGehee
Hope
Warren
Eudora
Denison
Whitesboro
Paris
TNER
Sherman
New Boston
Texarkana
El Dorado
DSRR
Hosston
Tallulah
Mineral Wells
DALLAS
Marshall
Shreveport
Monroe
Lovington
TNMR
Abilene
FORT WORTH
Everman
Lindale
Longview
Henderson
Big Spring
Odessa
Monahans
El Paso
Sierra Blanca
San Martine
Ballinger
Waco
Palestine
Natchez
MP/T&P joint trackage (Alexandria - New Orleans)
Alexandria
Eola
AKDN
Kinder
KCS
KCS
Baton Rouge
Valley Jct.
Huntsville
Round Rock
DeQuincy
Austin
Navasota
Hull
KCS
Beaumont
Lake Charles
Jefferson Island
Garden City
NEW ORLEANS
NOGC
Myrtle Grove
Empire
Thibodaux
Spring
HOUSTON
Baytown
Cedar Bayou
Texas City
Galveston
San Antonio
Angleton
Freeport
Dabney
Victoria
Crystal City
Bloomington
Long Mott
Carrizo Springs
Gardendale
Odem
Corpus Christi
Laredo
BOP
Rio Grande City
RVSG
Brownsville
0 50 100 150 200 miles
© 2023, Kalmbach Media Co., TRAINS; Robert Wegner
AKDN Acadiana
AKMD Arkansas Midland
BLRS Blacklands
BNSF Burlington Northern Santa Fe
BOP Border Pacific
DSRR Delta Southern
FSR Fort Smith
JGDR Jackson, Gordonville & Delta
K&O Kansas & Oklahoma
KCS Kansas City Southern
KYLE Kyle
MNA Missouri & Northern Arkansas
NOGC New Orleans & Gulf Coast
RVSG Rio Valley Switching
SKOL South Kansas & Oklahoma
TNER Texas Northeastern
TNMR Texas-New Mexico
MISSOURI PACIFIC SYSTEM, 1970/2004
MoPac proper, operated by UP
Texas & Pacific, operated by UP
Chicago & Eastern Illinois, operated by UP
Missouri-Illinois, operated by UP
MP system now operated by others
MP system lines abandoned

including Rock Island, Missouri Pacific, and Kansas City Southern—lines that too often had superior routes. These difficult conditions plagued the line despite its solid freight connections. The Katy was bankrupt when the United States Railroad Administration assumed operations of U.S. railroads during World War I. After it was restored to private ownership in 1920 it continued to struggle. In the 1920s, the railroad trimmed weaker routes and was reorganized in 1923 as the Missouri-Kansas-Texas Railroad. During the 1930s, it was under the direction of Matthew Sloan, who introduced a variety of improvements such as highway-competitive fast freights named the *Katy Komet* and the *Klipper*. In later years the Katy system consisted of more than a half dozen railways with the M-K-T at its core.

In the mid-20th century Katy lagged in investment in motive power. It never embraced simple articulateds, Super-Power, or any other late-steam-era innovations, having bought its last new steam engines in 1925. Its largest locomotives were 2-8-2 Mikados for freight and 4-6-2 Pacifics for passenger service. By the end of the World War II traffic surge, M-K-T's aged locomotive fleet was tired and its physical plant worn out. Desperate for new motive power, Katy undertook haphazard dieselization by ordering small batches of diesel-electrics from all the major builders. From EMD it bought a selection of F3s and F7s and a handful of E7 and E8s, plus GP7s and several kinds of switchers; from Alco it ordered a small fleet of PAs for passenger service and FAs for freight, along with RS3 road switchers. Baldwin supplied AS16 road switchers and DS4-4-1000 and S12 switchers, and Fairbanks-Morse supplied H16-44 road switchers.

Its rapidly assembled fleet of postwar diesels were largely worn out by the early 1960s, so the Katy replaced or repowered its diesels to keep ahead of the swell of traffic. The railroad had some of its Baldwin and Alco diesels rebuilt by Electro-Motive using its more-reliable 567 diesel engines, while retaining their bodies, trucks and electrical components. These odd hybrids served the railroad into the 1980s, with some surviving until the eve of the UP takeover.

The M-K-T was never a major passenger carrier. Among its best-remembered passenger trains was the *Katy Flyer*, which connected St. Louis, Dallas/Fort Worth, and San Antonio. In the late 1950s, under the administration of William Deramus III, the railroad modernized its freight services and cut passenger schedules to the bare minimum. Not long after John W. Barriger took over in 1965, Katy ran its last passenger train, with its small fleet of E units sold to Atlantic Coast Line.

Barriger wasted no time in making the railroad a more efficient freight carrier, and in 1969, the railroad was put under control of Katy Industries. Despite some difficulties, the railroad survived longer than both Rock Island and Missouri Pacific, other railroads that served the same region. Between 1943 and 1982, the M-K-T system was scaled back from 3,293 to, 2,211 miles, despite addition of some former Rock Island trackage operated as its Oklahoma-Kansas-Texas subsidiary. Among its most significant facilities were yards in Parsons, Kan., Bellmead (near Waco, Texas), and Denison, Texas.

After years of seeking a partner, Katy was finally swept up by the merger movement. In May 1988, a century after it was separated from Jay Gould's Missouri Pacific empire, Union Pacific acquired the venerable property; technically the Katy was merged into UP's Missouri Pacific subsidiary, and in August 1988 UP absorbed the M-K-T. While some trackage has since been pared back, the core of Katy's late-era route structure survives on the modern-day UP.

In 1952, MP E7 No. 7009 leads the *Texas Eagle* as it arrives at St. Louis during the morning rush hour. Note the Terminal Railroad Association of St. Louis Baldwin DS4-4-1000 switcher in the background alongside UP boxcars with the "Route of the Streamliners" logo. *Harold E. Williams*

Missouri Pacific Lines

Missouri Pacific had its origins in an 1849 Pacific Railroad charter that predicated a route from St. Louis to Kansas City and thence straight west over the Rockies to the West Coast. This visionary—but impractical—route never reached beyond the Great Plains. In 1851 the railroad began its ambitious push westward, built to the standard Missouri track gauge of 5 feet 6 inches. This proved impractical, and in 1869 the line was re-gauged to the North American standard of 4 feet 8½m inches and renamed the Pacific Railroad

In 1876, the company was reorganized as the Missouri Pacific, and by 1879 was under control of financier Jay Gould. Seeing great potential for MP, he favored this line among his other railroads and made it central to his railroad empire-building. Gould benefited the railroad not just through rapid expansion of its network, but by improving its infrastructure, operations, and customer base. In just a few years, he grew MP into an impressive regional system. After his death in 1893, Jay's son George used the MP system as a core property for his ambitious plan for a transcontinental empire. By that time MP had extended westward across the plains of Kansas and eastern Colorado to Pueblo to meet the Denver & Rio Grande Western, also Gould property. George's empire crumbled during World War I, and afterward MP secured an empire of its own starting in 1917 when it merged with its long-time affiliate, St. Louis, Iron Mountain & Southern (which operated lines extending south from St. Louis to Texas and Louisiana). In the 1920s, MP absorbed the International & Great Northern and took control of Texas & Pacific, another of its long-time affiliates.

Chartered to the West Coast, T&P, like MP, never got within a time zone of its named goal. The T&P ran from New Orleans to El Paso, Texas. Under MP control, T&P retained a degree of independence through the mid-20th century. It was famous for its early adoption of Lima Super-Power in the form of pioneering 2-10-4s—named the "Texas" type in its honor.

In 1930, the Van Sweringen brothers of Cleveland added MP to the growing portfolio of railroad properties controlled by their Alleghany Corporation. Like the Goulds, these financial wizards embraced empire-building visions of which MP was a late component that gave them transcontinental aspirations. Soon after controlling MP, they added Chicago & Eastern Illinois to their network. This addition not only gave the MP system access to Chicago but also offered a key link in the brothers' growing collection of railroads. However, the volatile financial landscape of the Great Depression and over-leveraged finances destroyed their empire. In 1933, MP entered bankruptcy and ended its Van Sweringen affiliation with C&EI. The brothers died in 1935 and 1936, by which time they were financially ruined. However, their Alleghany Corporation continued to exert an influence on railroad combinations for many years. MP didn't recover from bankruptcy until it was reorganized in 1956.

Starting in 1939, MP invested in a streamlined fleet of trains marketed as the *Eagles*. The first *Eagle* service consisted of two six-car sets, built by American Car & Foundry, operating between St. Louis, Kansas City, and Omaha. These were hauled by Electro-Motive E3 diesels specially styled for MP with rows of porthole windows along the sides of the locomotives.

Postwar, MP continued to expand its *Eagle* fleet. The *Texas Eagle* was improved with the addition of dome cars, connecting St. Louis with various cities in the south. Most exotic was its *Aztec Eagle,* which carried through cars from St. Louis to Mexico City. Despite its investment, like many railroads by the mid-1950s, MP's passenger services suffered from declining traffic and became unprofitable; yet through the 1950s the railroad operated the trains as a matter of pride. Efforts to attract more business included the introduction of low-cost sleeping cars.

In the early 1960s, under the extraordinary management of William Marbury and Downing Jenks, MP made rapid strides toward becoming a modern

Missouri Pacific was one of 25 railroads to buy Electro-Motive's game-changing model FT road diesel, a model easily identified by its row of four closely spaced porthole windows. *Robert A. Buck collection*

railroad. It was among the first large railroads to exit the passenger business. The railroad's late-era logo of a stylized fierce eagle profile paid tribute to its passenger trains years after the last trains were withdrawn. Jenks was an operational genius and invested in the railroad by improving its lines with continuous welded rail, deep ballast, and Centralized Traffic Control signaling and dispatching. To replace its early diesels, MP bought fleets of modern high-horsepower EMD diesels. MoPac promoted intermodal service and pioneered a computerized car-tracking system that set industry-wide precedents. Benefitting MP was a southwestern shift in American business in the 1960s that saw rapid economic growth in its service areas. By the mid-1970s, MP's southern region accounted for the largest share of the railroad's revenue, largely driven by increases in chemical traffic.

To prosper further, MP needed to expand. In the 1960s, MP and Louisville & Nashville vied for control of Chicago & Eastern Illinois. Both lines desired this minor carrier in order to reach Chicago. The railroads eventually negotiated a protracted arrangement that divided C&EI's route structure between them, with MP taking routes between Chicago and Thebes, Ill., to St. Louis. It wasn't until 1976 that MP formally merged with C&EI.

By this time, MP was ripe for merger itself. In 1981, MP agreed to merge with UP, an agreement that was approved by the ICC in September 1982. Immediately after the merger, MP in many ways remained the dominant force behind the combined

In 1925 Texas & Pacific was among the first to purchase Lima Super-Power steam locomotives, buying a fleet of 2-10-4s. These represented expansion of Lima's original 2-8-4 Berkshire design, and the two locomotive types shared many common specifications and equipment, including the prominent placement of an Elesco feedwater heater over the smokebox. No. 620 is at Shreveport, La., on Sept. 16, 1948. *John E. Pickett collection*

companies because key members of MP's management team, notably Dick Davidson, went on to assume the leadership of Union Pacific.

The complex nature of MP's network and traffic was contrary to UP's. Whereas UP's main line was a focused east-west trunk with its basic structure reaching from Council Bluffs to the Pacific (as described in Chapter 4), MP's system was a maze of lines connecting gateways and shipping across its service area. Initially, it was feared that combining UP and MP operations would be unwieldy. The UP's Kenefick had experienced first-hand the Penn Central merger meltdown a decade earlier, which was caused in part by difficulties in forcing together the disparate Pennsylvania and New York Central networks and management teams. Kenefick learned from that, and the public image and operations of the two railroads remained separate for a few years after the merger. MoPac retained its distinctive blue livery on locomotives until 1984, and for a few years after that its new and repainted locomotives—although dressed in UP's Armor yellow and gray—still featured "MISSOURI PACIFIC" lettering.

Southern Pacific

Southern Pacific was the most complicated railroad in the West. It originated with the desire for a transcontinental link across the Sierras, and gradually evolved to include dozens of companies in intricate—and sometimes convoluted—combinations. In the late 1850s and early 1860s, railroad visionary

The Jefferson City local still embraced a late-era Missouri Pacific appearance nearly six years after MP merged with UP. The train works westward, parallel to the former Route 66 near Pacific, Mo., on Nov. 27, 1988. *Scott Muskopf*

Theodore D. Judah surveyed a railroad crossing of the Sierra Nevada mountains via Donner Pass, and convinced four of Sacramento's most successful business owners—Collis P. Huntington, Leland Stanford, Charles Crocker, and Mark Hopkins (later known as the "Big Four")—to back his idea. Together they created the Central Pacific Railroad. Keys to their success were the various talents of the Big Four. Huntington was the master of business and the visionary behind the Big Four dealings. He outlived the others and continued to dominate the business until his death in 1900. Stanford was a politician, conveniently elected Governor of California about the time he became involved with the railroad. Crocker organized construction, and Hopkins served as accountant.

Critical to their transcontinental dream was the passage of the Pacific Railroad Act of July 1862, which by providing federal land grants and cash incentives, encouraged and paid for the railroad's early construction. Judah was the catalyst that put the railroad in motion. He was a multitalented individual with an intense personality and was obsessed with his railroad vision. He personally lobbied in Washington for passage of the Pacific Railroad Act, but quickly became dissatisfied with the Big Four's business dealings. The Big Four forced Judah out before any track was built. Judah contracted tropical fever traveling from California to the East Coast via Panama, in what was a last ditch effort to take back control of the railroad. He died in New York in November 1863 at age 37. The peak above the line at Donner summit is named for him.

The Central Pacific began construction at Sacramento in January 1863, building eastward toward Donner Pass. Construction was initially slow and suffered delays from shortages of labor and material, in part because of the exceptional difficulties reaching California, plus a dearth of local

This eastbound UP freight still had an all-Missouri Pacific look on Nov. 21, 1987, as it passed the 1893-built MP station in Kirkwood, Mo. The area in the foreground was once a small yard and turntable for commuter trains. *Scott Muskopf*

industry and the ongoing effects of the Civil War. By 1865, the CP had only built to the Sierra foothills near Auburn, Calif., 35 miles east from where it started. Crocker, who was overseeing construction, found a bold solution by hiring Chinese immigrants to help build the railroad. Ultimately, an estimated 14,000 Chinese laborers worked for CP, including many recruited from mainland China. The mountain going was slow and tough, boring through solid rock to establish the right-of-way. The railroad approached Donner Summit in July 1867, and the Sierra crossing was open by May 1868. Crocker's work gangs then began racing eastward across the Nevada and Utah deserts against Union Pacific's westward construction teams.

The Golden Spike ceremony at Promontory marked the meeting of CP and UP, but it was hardly the end of the race. In many ways it was just a stepping stone for the Big Four, who over the next 30 years connected numerous points in California, Oregon, and across the Southwest by building, financing, leasing, and otherwise controlling every railroad company within their grasp. Savvy masters of 19th-century business, the Big Four effectively dominated transportation in the state of California and adjacent areas.

While Central Pacific was at the core of their burgeoning empire, their organization's future namesake company, Southern Pacific, began as the San Francisco & San Jose, which ran its first trains in June 1864. This line emerged as a potential competitor to Central Pacific in 1866 when its principals incorporated the Southern Pacific, which proposed connecting San Francisco to San Diego via a minor waterfront settlement called Los Angeles.

Of greater concern to the Big Four was that Congress had authorized Southern Pacific as the western leg of a southern transcontinental railroad, which posed a

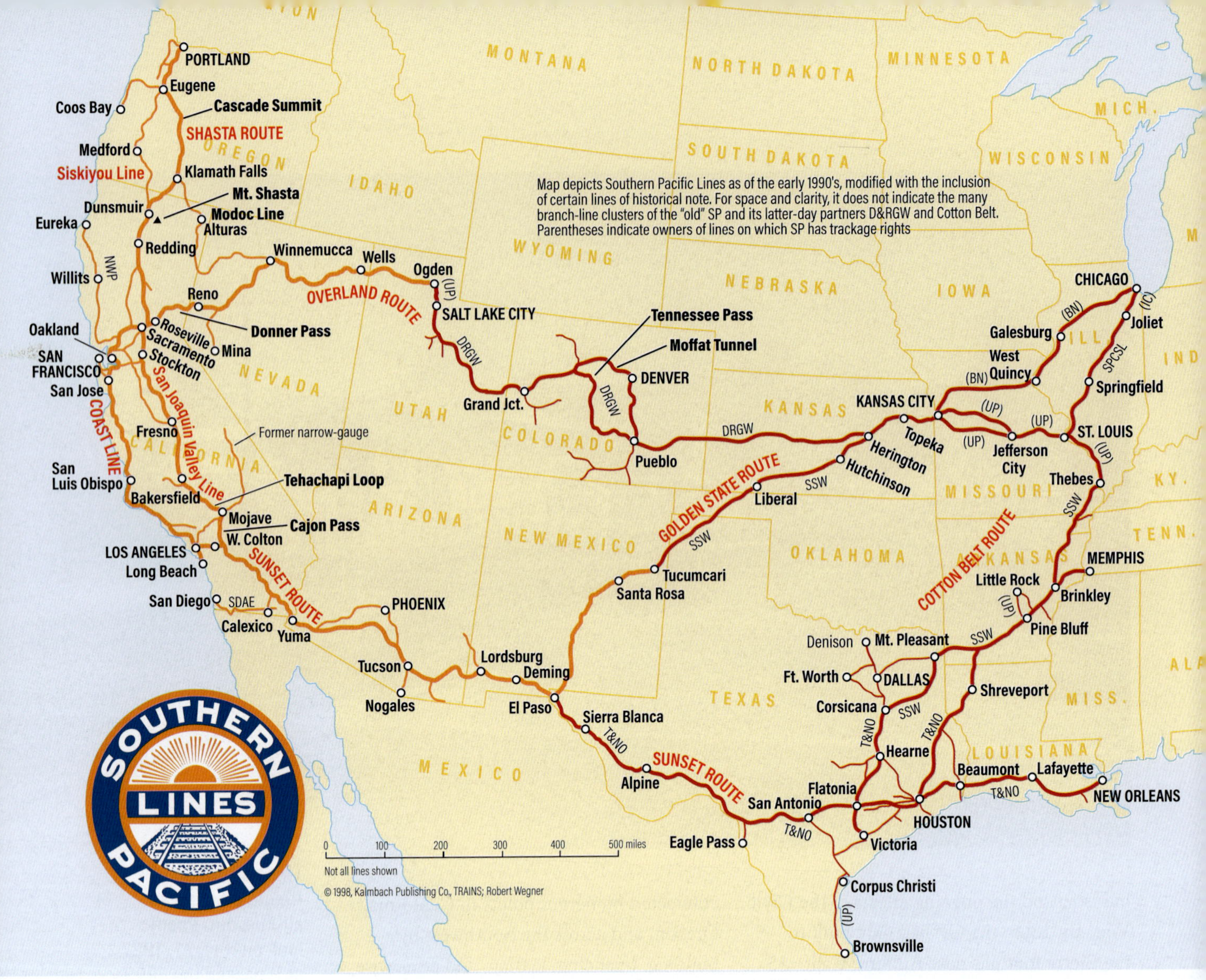

serious threat to CP. The SP's planners envisioned building southeast from San Jose to Gilroy, Calif., over the rugged Pacheco Pass, then across the San Joaquin Valley and over the Tehachapis to span the Mojave desert to a point near the Colorado River where it would meet the Atlantic & Pacific, which was chartered to build west.

In an oft-repeated pattern of acquisition and control, before long the SP became part of the Big Four's transportation portfolio. Although interested in a Southern transcon line, the Big Four found that SP's proposed Pacheco Pass crossing impractical, so they instead built from a connection with one of its existing lines, then through the San Joaquin Valley toward Bakersfield, Calif. From there, SP's grading engineer William Hood built a sinuous crossing of the Tehachapi mountains. To maintain a steady gradient, Hood included a complete 360-degree spiral at Walong, Calif.: the world famous railroad landmark known as "Tehachapi Loop." Hood proved to be among the finest railroad construction engineers in the West. He was promoted to chief engineer in 1883 and served SP into the 1920s.

Southern Pacific reached Los Angeles on Sept. 5, 1876, and in 1884 the Big Four reorganized myriad properties under their control under the name Southern Pacific Company. The Central Pacific was formally leased to the SP in 1885, effectively ending it as an operating entity (although CP wouldn't be formally merged into SP until 1959). By 1887, the Big Four completed their first Oregon route, using Hood's hastily built Siskiyou Line that employed a series of 3% grades and tortuous curves to wind over the mountains. When Huntington died in 1900, SP controlled more than 8,000 miles of railroad in the U.S. and Mexico, and was still expanding. In 1901, SP closed the last gap on its Coast Line, which served as its second San Francisco-Los Angeles main line, crossing the Coast Range via the Cuesta ascent near San Luis Obispo, Calif.

Union Pacific's E. H. Harriman had long had his eyes on the Central Pacific route, and saw Huntington's death as his opportunity to act. Harriman acquired 45% control of SP in 1901, and famously remarked, "We have bought not only a railroad, but an empire." A master of contemporary business management, he empowered his officers to make a detailed assessment of his new property. Following the advice of SP's able General Manager, Julius Kruttschnitt, Harriman authorized tens of millions of dollars for massive engineering improvements aimed to improve traffic flow and lower operating costs. This included building a new Bayshore Cutoff to improve access to San Francisco; the Montalvo Cutoff by way of Santa Susana Pass to shorten the Coast Line route; and double-tracking CP's Overland Route over Donner that interchanged with UP at Ogden.

The SP continued to expand under Harriman, buying into the Los Angeles-centered Pacific Electric interurban empire in 1903 and helping build the San Diego & Eastern along the California-Mexico border (which later became SP's San Diego & Arizona Eastern subsidiary). The SP and Santa Fe cooperated beginning in 1907 with the Northwestern Pacific, which had consolidated smaller railroads and ran north of San Francisco into the redwoods territory. The NWP completed its main line to Eureka, Calif., in 1914, and in 1927 SP assumed complete control of the line, operating it as subsidiary.

However, Harriman's plans to fully unify UP and SP were foiled by the anti-trust initiatives that viewed railroad mergers as uncompetitive, and so the two railroads were separated in a series of protracted legal battles that weren't fully resolved until the 1920s.

In the mid-1920s, freed from the uncertainty of USRA control and legal proceedings, the now-independent SP made a series of major late steam-era improvements. It finally completed the Donner Pass double-tracking that had begun under Harriman. Significant projects involved building completely new alignments, including grading a much-improved summit crossing for westbound trains that required boring a two-mile summit tunnel east of Norden, Calif. SP built the long-planned Natron Cutoff to complete a better route from northern California to Oregon. Construction began in September 1923, and the line was opened in February 1926. SP's new Cascade route diverged from the Siskiyou Line at Black Butte, Calif., near the base of California's Mount Shasta. The crowning achievement was its serpentine crossing of Oregon's Pengra Pass, where the line passes through a dozen tunnels and numerous snow sheds. Although both the Siskiyou and Cascade lines served SP as through routes until the early 1990s, the Cascade route was superior and carried the lion's share of freight, leaving the Siskiyou primarily for local traffic. The Cascade route was nearly 24-miles shorter, had fewer curves, and its maximum grade of 1.8% was far better than the 3% maximum on the Siskiyou.

The railroad's final new steam-era construction project was the Alturas Cutoff, better known as the Modoc line in later years, which opened in 1929. This combined portions of the old Nevada-California-Oregon narrow gauge and new construction to provide a direct shortcut

On Sept. 20, 1981, duty-worn Cotton Belt GP20 No. 4141 blurs through the rice fields between Dayton and Crosby, Texas, with symbol freight BTHO-M (Beaumont to Houston Manifest). This is on SP's famed Sunset Route between Los Angles and New Orleans. *Tom Kline*

connection from Klamath Falls, Ore., to the CP Overland Route in Nevada. Almost exclusively a freight line, it crossed some of most sparsely populated areas of California.

That era also included several significant acquisitions for SP. In 1924, SP obtained ICC approval to buy the El Paso & Southwestern, which connected with Texas & Pacific at El Paso, Texas and the Rock Island at Tucumcari, N.M. The Southern Pacific marketed Rock Island's gateway as the "Golden State Route." This was a slick move for SP, since it provided an alternative to the UP Ogden interchange: SP was no longer beholden to UP for transcontinental traffic, while potential comptetition was sealed off.

Perhaps SP's most-significant post-Harriman expansion occurred in 1932 when it gained control of the St. Louis Southwestern (commonly known as the Cotton Belt), a railroad that had floundered during the early 1900s. The Cotton Belt ran, as its official name indicated, southwesterly from St. Louis via Pine Bluff, Ark., to Dallas/Fort Worth, Texas, with branches to Memphis, Tenn., Shreveport, La., and southeastern Texas. This provided SP access to the gateway cities of Memphis and St. Louis and tapped important petrochemical and agricultural traffic.

On June 29, 1955, John E. Pickett paced Southern Pacific 4-6-0 No. 2248 leading an eastbound fire-service water train near Roseville, Calif. The SP operated water trains into the 1990s to mitigate the risk of fire along its lines.
John E. Pickett

Opposite Top: Southern Pacific was famous for its unique oil-burning Cab-Forward articulated steam locomotives. They were designed to avoid crew asphyxiation during operation through tunnels and snowsheds at high altitude in the California Sierras. No. 4003 was one of the earliest of the design. Built by Baldwin as a Mallet compound in 1909, it's pictured in March 1951 after conversion to simple operation.
John E. Pickett

Santa Fe and Southern Pacific anticipated approval of their merger proposal and painted locomotives in their new corporate scheme, only to have the ICC soundly reject the proposed combination. On Feb. 16, 1987, SP SD9 No. 4418 works the *Oxnard Flyer* at Goleta, Calif., wearing the bright colors of a merger that would never be.
Thomas L. Carver

Under SP control, Cotton Belt was allowed a high degree of autonomy, and locomotives and equipment continued to be lettered for the line into the 1990s. Cotton Belt's most famous trains were its *Blue Streak* fast freights, which started as merchandise (less-than-carload) trains and eventually expanded to carry automotive, intermodal, and other priority traffic. Under the SP some schedules were extended via the Sunset Route to serve Los Angeles.

SP's freight business flourished as California's economy grew. By contrast, SP's extensive passenger network was among the first seriously threatened by the advent of public highways and the automobile culture, and it faced declining business in some areas prior to World War I. In the mid-1930s, SP embraced modern streamlined design with its steam-powered *Daylight.* This brightly painted train connected San Francisco and Los Angeles via the Coast Line. The *Daylight's* success inspired a family of similar trains to attract passengers back to the rails. Following an unprecedented surge in passenger traffic during World War II, SP made a massive investment in new streamliners. On the San Francisco-Portland, Ore., run, SP introduced its new diesel-led *Shasta Daylight* in 1949, followed by the overnight *Cascade* in 1950. It also re-equipped its famed *Sunset Limited* that served the Los Angeles-New Orleans Sunset Route. By the late 1950s, passenger traffic was on the decline, and many trains were downgraded and eliminated; what was left went into Amtrak in 1971.

Southern Pacific began dieselizing in the 1940s and ran its last domestic steam locomotive in 1957. During the 1950s and 1960s, SP transformed its network into a modern freight carrier, installing Centralized Traffic Control over many of its busiest routes. To expedite movements through Los Angeles, it built a new freight-only cutoff between Palmdale and West Colton, Calif., by way of Cajon Pass that opened in 1967. Despite innovative solutions and robust traffic, SP was struggling financially by the mid-1970s, and under the administration of Benjamin Biaggiani, SP discussed merger possibilities with Union Pacific, but at the time UP wasn't interested.

In 1980, Santa Fe began merger talks with SP but the railroads were unable to come to agreement on how to handle SP's substantial real estate holdings and terminated discussions. Three years later, Santa Fe resumed talks with SP and by the end of the 1983, the railroads' holding companies merged to form Santa Fe Southern Pacific Corporation, but the railroads remained independent while awaiting regulatory approval from the ICC. Based on what had been viewed as a favorable climate for mergers in the West, SP and Santa Fe anticipated the ICC's blessing and began painting locomotives in new red and yellow corporate scheme. It was a shock to the railroads and many industry observers when in 1986 the ICC firmly denied the merger on the basis of being anticompetitive. Despite appeals, the deal was dead; as a result SFSP Corporation was forced to dispose of SP, which by this time had been in limbo for years and was in relatively poor shape compared to its competitors, which now again included the Santa Fe.

In 1988, Anschutz Corporation, which owned Denver & Rio Grande Western, acquired control of SP, putting the two railroads under common ownership. SP then sought through routes to Chicago, and in 1989 acquired the old Alton route between St. Louis and Joliet, Ill. (which had been spun off by Illinois Central Gulf a few years earlier), including trackage rights over Illinois Central to Chicago. A year later SP secured a second Chicago connection via trackage rights over Burlington Northern between Kansas City and Chicago. Finally, as a condition of the 1995 Burlington Northern-Santa Fe merger, SP obtained a third route to Chicago. During the 1980s

Southern Pacific SD40T-2 No. 8248 leads an eastbound train across the Harahan Bridge over the Mississippi River on the Cotton Belt toward Memphis, Tenn., on Oct. 14, 1993. This double-track bridge, nearly 5,000 feet long, was built by a group of railroads including St. Louis Southwestern; SSW became part of UP in 1996. *Tom Kline*

New Southern Pacific SD70M No. 9806 leads an eastbound freight at Mojave, Calif. The Espee's order of 25 SD70Ms (Nos. 9800-9824) was delivered in 1996, shortly before SP merged with UP.
Thomas L. Carver

Southern Pacific received the first of its 101 Dash 9-44CWs from GE in spring 1994. A pair of these modern safety cab-equipped, 4,400-hp diesels make their first westbound trip over Donner Pass on June 10, 1994.
Brian Solomon

In the early 1950s, Southern Pacific MT-3 class 4-8-2 No. 4341 leads second No. 563—an Overland route freight consisting of empty Pacific Fruit Express reefers returning west to Roseville, Calif. The train is crossing a Harriman-era standard truss bridge over the Truckee River near Thisby, Nev. The SP's 4-8-2s were built for passenger service but ended up working fast freights after World War II. *John E. Pickett*

On Sept. 4, 1939, Western Pacific 2-8-8-2 No. 254 works an eastbound freight in the Feather River Canyon at milepost 280. The telltale over the train warns of the approach to Tunnel No. 31. Beyond is Tunnel No. 32, which is located immediately west of the famous Spanish Fork Bridge at Keddie, Calif. *Robert A. Buck collection*

and early 1990s, SP spun off many of its secondary routes, with most going to short lines that could feed SP traffic. Roughly coinciding with consummation of the BNSF merger in 1995, UP announced its intent to buy SP (including Rio Grande and Cotton Belt), and the two railroad systems were merged on Sept. 11, 1996.

Western Pacific

The Western Pacific was the last transcontinental route completed in the United States. It was finished a half century after Central Pacific and Union Pacific's pioneering transcon, a route along which WP largely ran parallel. George Gould had inherited key elements of his father's railroad empire including Wabash, Missouri Pacific, and Denver & Rio Grande Western, a network that effectively connected Buffalo, N.Y. with Salt Lake City. Unlike the 19th-century "transcontinentals" that connected lines in the Midwest with the Pacific, George envisioned a true transcontinental railway that reached all the way from coast to coast. To fulfill this goal, he aimed to fill in the gaps in his network. Despite the risks of penetrating the territory of some of the largest and most-influential railroad systems, Gould undertook ambitious plans for new construction. To bridge the largest gap between Salt Lake City and the Pacific coast, Gould mortgaged the D&RGW to fund the all-new Western Pacific Railway to reach San Francisco Bay.

Gould's WP was formed in 1903, establishing its headquarters in San Francisco. While some formative work had already been undertaken, construction officially began opposite San Francisco on the Oakland, Calif., waterfront in 1906 and progressed rapidly, with crews working simultaneously along several points of the route. WP's line angled southeast from Oakland, following SP's Central Pacific line through Niles Canyon, then over Altamont Pass to the San Joaquin Valley, where the railroad followed a north-south alignment from Stockton through Sacramento to Oroville, Calif. It then penetrated the Sierra Nevadas by building along the north and middle forks of the twisting and rugged Feather River Canyon.

It crossed a low saddle of the Sierras at Beckwourth Pass (named for the western explorer who discovered the pass) and continued east across some of the driest and remotest portions of the northern Nevada desert by way of Sand Pass and Gerlach to Winnemucca, Nev., where it again ran roughly parallel with the Central Pacific to Wells, Nev. To reach Salt Lake City, WP built along a new alignment south of CP's line, via Shafter, Nev., and over Silver Zone Pass via the winding Arnold Loop into Utah at Wendover, Utah, then across the desolate salt flats south of Great Salt Lake.

Unlike early transcontinental lines, where hasty, shoddy construction was tolerated to get the railroad finished quickly, Gould's WP was a showcase for modern construction. Its grades were relatively gentle, made possible by numerous steel viaducts and long tunnels. It was 140 miles longer than SP's route over Donner Pass, but crossed a lower summit that avoided the worst of the Sierra's deep snowfalls. The most difficult construction was through Feather River Canyon. The deep and rugged rocky cleft of the north fork of the river east of Oroville had been considered since the 1860s as the path of a transcontinental line, but remained remote and unsettled until WP construction began. *The Railway and Engineering Review* reported in March 1910 that when WP surveyed the line there was "no means of transportation in the canyon—not even a pack trail." WP first needed to build a wagon road before starting on the railroad. Ultimately the line required 28 tunnels just between Oroville and Keddie, Calif., as well as numerous trestles. East of Keddie, the railroad bored several very long tunnels. The longest, at Spring Garden, Calif., was

A long Western Pacific eastbound freight crosses over itself at the famous Williams Loop, located in the Middle Fork of the Feather River Canyon. The loop allowed the railroad to limit its gradient to 1%, giving the line a much easier ascent of the Sierras then the parallel Southern Pacific crossing over Donner Pass. GE U23B No. 2261 leads the train on Oct. 25, 1972. *Brian Jennison*

7,306 feet long; WP's summit tunnel at Beckwourth Pass measured 6,006 feet.

When completed in November 1909, Gould's vision connected the dots on a map but failed to tap online traffic, and the WP was little more than a long, low-grade branch to the Pacific. In the days when carload traffic accounted for the lion's share of freight, WP lacked the reach to deliver customers' cars. The high cost of construction, combined with lack of traffic, contributed to Gould's financial collapse and led to WP's bankruptcy. On the eve of American involvement in World War I, WP was reorganized as the Western Pacific Railroad—a company jointly owned by Denver & Rio Grande Western and Missouri Pacific. This eliminated some challenging limitations imposed by its original charter, freeing WP to obtain necessary feeders.

During the War, the USRA's period of control coordinated operations on WP and SP main lines across central Nevada. Between Winnemucca and Wells, Nev., these parallel but non-adjacent single-track main lines were organized as a paired-track arrangement that effectively gave both railroads the benefits of directional double-track by using one main eastbound and the other west. During this same time, WP's new administration acquired lines in California's San Joaquin Valley, notably the Tidewater Southern, in 1917. In 1921, WP acquired Sacramento Northern's interurban empire, and later melded this with another electric line, the Oakland, Antioch & Eastern. This formed an alternative route between Sacramento and the Bay Area but required a ferry over the San Joaquin River between the two disconnected lines.

In the late 1920s, financier Arthur C. James bought control of WP and coordinated with Great Northern to build one of the last important freight corridors in the far West, known as the "Inside Gateway." The WP built northward from Keddie, where the new line diverged from the main line on a junction situated on Spanish Creek Trestle; the western leg of the famous Keddie Wye. Continuing north, WP's line met Great Northern's extension at Bieber, Calif., in 1931.

By 1949, WP's freight revenue was 20 times greater than passenger receipts, yet WP is best remembered by the general public for its famous Budd-built streamlined domeliner, the *California Zephyr,* introduced that year. The train was operated between Chicago and Oakland in conjunction with the Burlington and Rio Grande and was popular for its daylight passage through the scenic Feather River Canyon. By 1970, the *Cal Zephyr* was a drain on WP's meager resources and was discontinued a

An eastbound Western Pacific freight plies the desolate main line across the salt flats between Wendover and Knolls, Utah. *Mel Patrick*

Western Pacific's San Jose Turn is at the Redmond Cut on California's Altamont Pass on Nov. 15, 1976. This quartet of F7s regularly worked the SJT, typically departing Stockton, Calif., around 1 p.m. and reaching Altamont Pass in the early afternoon. *Brian Jennison*

year before Amtrak assumed responsibility for most remaining American intercity passenger service. Today's Amtrak train of the same name runs via the shorter route over Donner Pass and so misses the Feather River Canyon line, which remains a freight-only route.

The Western Pacific was among the original buyers of Electro-Motive's pioneering FT road freight diesel, and except for a few Alco and Baldwin switchers, it largely dieselized with EMD products. In the 1960s and 1970s, it augmented its diesel fleet with nine GE U30Bs and 15 U23Bs. Unlike most other Western railroads, WP didn't buy six-axle diesels.

In the early 1960s, the construction of the Oroville Dam along the North Fork of Feather River required a significant line relocation and abandonment of 27 miles of the original route, much of it flooded by the new Lake Oroville reservoir. WP's new line was opened in 1962 and included some substantial late-era railroad construction including two long tunnels (No. 8 measured 8,856 feet) and a massive parabolic concrete bridge over the North Fork branch of the river deep in the Feather River Canyon.

Southern Pacific and Santa Fe both considered merging WP in the early 1960s without success. WP remained independent until UP absorbed it in 1982. Since that time it has served as an important freight route. UP's 1996 merger with SP facilitated BNSF ownership of the Inside Gateway north from Keddie while granting BNSF trackage rights over most of the former WP, including through the Feather River Canyon.

CHAPTER 3

PASSENGER TRAINS

The Union pacific operated a large fleet of long-distance trains and was a pioneer in the diesel streamliner

Union Pacific E9 No. 950 leads a streamlined consist of the *Portland Rose* at Denver on June 15, 1968. The E unit was built in May 1955. Even as passenger train routes were being curtailed on the eve of Amtrak, UP's trains continued to have a classic, well-maintained appearance.
J. David Ingles

Passenger trains were a key in settling the western U.S., as they cut months from the time required to travel by wagon. Many early Union Pacific passengers were awed by the experience of seeing the West for the first time.

In 1884, Frederick E. Shearer compiled *The Pacific Tourist,* which served as a guidebook for the western traveler. A week-long journey riding in a series of bouncy, unheated, non-air-conditioned wooden railway cars was viewed as a vehicle of optimism. The excitement of travel provided otherwise-fatigued passengers with the energy to overcome the discomforts of early railway travel, which by any measure was an improvement over all the alternatives. And, Shearer determined that the Union Pacific was the best way West.

Union Pacific's primary trunk line was a key component of the Overland Route. It emerged as the main western passenger route for the U.S., hosting many named trains. For more than a half century, UP's flagship trains on this line carried train numbers 1 and 2, symbolic of their importance to the railroad. Many trains were operated in conjunction with Central Pacific (later Southern Pacific), to reach California. In the early years, transcontinental service was simply called the *Express.* Later they were known as the *Pacific Express* (westbound) and *Atlantic Express* (eastbound). After 1906, the westbound train was known as the *China & Japan Express.*

Among the plushest decorated trains catering to wealthy travelers was the *Overland Flyer* inaugurated in 1887.

The more famous *Overland Limited* began service in 1896, connecting Chicago to the Bay Area. In its day it was among the most-recognized named trains in America, and was simply known to passengers as the *Overland*. In 1902, following Harriman control of UP and SP, the train was upgraded with the latest in modern passenger equipment, including rubber tiles on the observation car platform and on-board telephones that could be plugged into the network during stops at main stations.

Harriman was focused on safety, so this was among the first trains equipped with steel-framed cars, which in the event of derailments or collisions were vastly safer than traditional all-wood cars. This coincided with other safety features, notably the adoption of automatic block signals that helped prevent rear-end crashes and improvements to the Overland Route track structure itself. Long stretches of the Central Pacific were rebuilt, with segments relocated to reduce curvature and gradient. The Harriman administration oversaw construction of the Lucin Cutoff, complete with a long trestle across the Great Salt Lake that completely bypassed the original line through Promontory Summit. These changes, together with improved locomotives and other equipment, shortened travel times between Council Bluffs, Iowa, and Oakland, Calif. By the mid-1920s, the train operated on a 58-hour schedule between Chicago and San Francisco.

After World War I, Union Pacific placed increasing emphasis on its transcontinental trains as local passenger business gradually diminished with improvements to parallel roads and the rise of the highway culture. During the 1920s and '30s, UP was compelled by greater competition—both from highways and other railroads—to speed up and improve its long-haul trains. This would be reflected in part by the development of its streamlined trains (see below) and by improvements to traditional trains, which continued to carry the bulk of its passengers for many years. Following World War II, the Overland Route finally offered a true transcontinental service when it began carrying through sleeping cars to and from both New York City and Washington D.C.

Beyond the Overland

The Overland trunk allowed UP to reach several western cities via connecting

Opposite: Historically, Union Pacific locomotive number boards displayed train numbers rather than locomotive numbers. On July 5, 1951, class FEF No. 823 leads the first section of train No. 6, the eastbound *Mail & Express*, at Hermosa, Wyo. Train 6 ran from Los Angeles to Omaha, carrying U. S. Mail and Railway Express Agency shipments at the head end with passenger cars at the back. *George C. Corey*

Union Pacific McKeen railcar M-4 rests between runs at Boulder, Colo., on Dec. 14, 1940. This car handled local service between Denver and Boulder. *Howard I. Kinney*

Union Pacific M-24 was one of the final McKeen cars. Built in December 1917, it was converted into a gas-electric in 1928 (with a Winton engine) to improve reliability. Later painted Armour yellow, it was also one of the last McKeens on the roster and was destroyed in a wreck in 1948.
Trains collection

lines and partnerships. Among the famous trains of the steam era were the *Portland Rose* (train Nos. 17 westbound and 18 eastbound), serving as UP's premier Chicago-Oregon service with connections at the western end to Tacoma, Wash., and Seattle and at its eastern end to Denver and Kansas City, and the *Los Angeles Limited,* which was the backbone of the Chicago-Los Angeles route.

The Union Pacific-Chicago & North Western partnership competed in the Chicago-Denver market against Rock Island and Chicago, Burlington & Quincy. In the Roaring Twenties, UP-C&NW introduced the *Columbine,* a classy service named for Colorado's state flower. The train's heavyweight, open-ended observation car carried a drumhead with an image of the popular blossom; on May 15, 1927, the governor of Colorado presided over the naming of the new train.

Less glamorous but more versatile than UP's other posh through trains was its *Pacific Limited,* a workhorse series of trains that via myriad connections and through cars served dozens of smaller cities and towns along the Overland Route. It wasn't one train, but many: In the timetable, the *Pacific Limited* comprised train Nos. 21, 23, and 25 westbound and Nos. 22, 24, and 26 eastbound. They connected Chicago with Portland, Ore., San Francisco, and Los Angeles, with sections from Kansas City to Denver that connected with the primary train at Cheyenne, Wyo. In addition, it carried through cars from Portland to Salt Lake City via Pocatello, Idaho. Unlike UP's faster transcontinental trains, the *Pacific Limited* stopped frequently, pausing at more than 40 stations across Nebraska alone. While many transcontinental passengers avoided this train, it was the vehicle of choice for passengers living along the line.

MCKEEN MOTOR COMPANY

In 1902, E.H. Harriman appointed William R. McKeen Jr., a young, fashionable, educated man from Indiana, as Union Pacific's superintendent of motive power and machinery. Two years into his post, Harriman sought McKeen's attention in finding a solution to UP's growing branchline traffic problem. Comparatively high costs combined with low traffic were threatening the economic sustainability of many branches, especially in the face of competition from electric interurban railways. Harriman's idea was visionary, but not original. He was inspired by U.S. Navy's recent adoption of gasoline-engine torpedo boats, and wondered if railcars powered by internal combustion could offer an inexpensive solution. McKeen embraced Harriman's vision and took it a few steps further by developing a novel lightweight, aerodynamic railcar powered by a primitive gasoline engine.

McKeen moved quickly, investigating and experimenting in motor car design, paying close attention to advances in both Europe and America while developing his own ideas. Working at UP's Omaha Shops, he produced a wood-body prototype in early 1905, followed by a second prototype a few months later with a light steel-truss body that established important precedents for his later production. Based in part on the distinctive design of his prototype, McKeen applied for a patent (issued in 1910) for a gasoline railcar that used a truss-frame body for strength and rigidity with a novel wedge-shaped nose designed to minimize wind resistance and improve adhesion at higher speeds. According to his patent, the nose would "utilize the wind pressure in driving the car toward the track."

McKeen's early railcars were built for Union Pacific and were powered by a 100-hp gasoline engine (later cars used larger engines). Early cars featured small rectangular windows, but the body shape evolved, and classic McKeen cars featured side porthole windows. This defining stylistic feature was first applied in early 1907 on a car constructed for the Erie Railroad.

Under the wing of Union Pacific, the McKeen Motor Company was launched on July 1, 1908. With Harriman's nod, UP allocated to McKeen the North Shop complex in Omaha. Harriman's railroads supported McKeen by placing significant orders for rail motor cars. By 1917, the company had built more than 150 railcars for several railroads across North America, as well as lines in Australia. However, the cars were plagued with mechanical problems. Unlike most later gasoline cars that employed an electric transmission, McKeen used a mechanical transmission which was prone to failure. Although the Harriman Roads invested in many cars, McKeen had few repeat customers. In 1920, Union Pacific assumed the assets of the failed venture.

While the motor car company failed commercially, it proved to be an important training exercise for Arthur H. Fetters, who worked closely with McKeen and who continued to study internal combustion engines; in the 1930s, Fetters was instrumental in the development of UP's early streamlined trains. Further, Edward G. Budd worked closely with the McKeen company on the structural details of the steel railcar bodies. In the 1930s, Budd emerged as one of the pioneers of streamlined train design, and the Budd Co. became one of the major builders of lightweight railroad passenger cars.

Diesel streamliners

In February 1934, UP debuted America's first internal-combustion streamlined passenger train, a Pullman-built, three-car articulated train powered by a Winton distillate engine. It was originally known as the *Streamliner*, and carried the number M10000. This train toured the U.S. and was among the precursors in the development of Electro-Motive's diesel-electric locomotives. The train's success ultimately led Union Pacific to invest in a fleet of diesel-electric streamlined trains.

The revolutionary M10000 awed the American public. The train was the product of UP's need to address its sagging passenger business. By the early 1930s, the combined effects of automobile

The cover of this Union Pacific brochure promotes its 1934 Pullman-built *Streamliner.* This sleek, fast, and compact diesel train changed the way UP and its passengers viewed rail travel. The UP's M10000 was later assigned to work as the *City of Salina.* *Solomon collection*

technology, public investment in modern paved intercity roads, and the effects of the Great Depression devastated railroad ridership nationwide. The situation was so dire that UP investigated abandoning its passenger services altogether, but deemed this unacceptable to the public because railroads were expected to provide passenger trains, not withstanding poor ridership and declining revenues. Union Pacific hoped to attract public interest and reduce operating costs with new trains. Conventional steam-hauled heavyweight trains were the backbone of intercity travel, but the advent

Union Pacific's Pullman-built M10001 entered regular service in May 1935 as the *City of Portland* running on a weekly schedule between Chicago and its namesake city. The train was built in 1934 and was powered by a 900-hp Winton 201A diesel engine. *Brian Solomon collection*

of modern automobiles and air travel made steam trains seem outmoded. Union Pacific wanted to entice passengers with modern trains that were not just faster, but also fashionable and fun to ride.

The UP recognized that the motive-power answer could be found with its competition. The railroad had studied the solution since Harriman's time: those ill-fated McKeen railcars along with more-common (and more-successful) gas-electrics from Electro-Motive and other builders held the answer. In the 1920s, before the drastic declines of the depression, Union Pacific enabled its general mechanical engineer, Arthur H. Fetters (see the sidebar on McKeen on page 79), to further his study of engine design. Fetters researched petroleum-fueled engine design, traveled to Europe to learn about diesel developments there, and reported back to Omaha. Ultimately his research helped transform the American passenger train while shaping UP efforts to acquire the first high-speed, lightweight, internal-combustion passenger train in 1934.

In 1932, Wagen und Maschinenbau AG in Germany built the world's first commercial high-speed diesel train using an articulated, two-section streamlined diesel-electric railcar powered by twin diesel engines, with aerodynamic design based on an experimental train called the Rail Zeppelin.

The two Pullman-built *City of Denver* sets featured a different streamlining treatment than the original three UP streamliners. This train took its styling from contemporary General Motors automobile design, carried heralds of both UP and C&NW, and was similar to the 1936 *City of San Francisco* train set. *Union Pacific*

The *City of San Francisco* made its debut in 1936 as a once-a-week streamliner on the Chicago-Oakland, Calif., run. In January 1938, after a little more than 18-months, this original train set was supplanted by a new *City of San Francisco* train with greater capacity and superior passenger comfort, hauled by custom-styled Electro-Motive E2 diesels. *Electro-Motive Corp.*

During the late 1920s the U.S. Navy had encouraged internal-combustion engine research to produce compact powerful engines suited for submarines. Among the leaders in engine design was Winton Engine Co. Winton had been an engine supplier for Electro-Motive's gas-electric railcars. In 1930, General Motors purchased both Winton and Electro-Motive, setting the stage for crucial advances in locomotive engine design. The Century of Progress exposition in Chicago in 1933 brought together GM, Union Pacific, and Pullman; UP's principal competitor, the Chicago, Burlington & Quincy, followed a similar path, and the two railroads raced to debut America's first streamlined train.

The UP and Pullman collaborated closely. UP's vice president of engineering, E.E. Adams, took charge of train design, and Pullman worked with the University of Michigan to perfect an aerodynamic shape. Ultimately, the resulting train presented a sharp contrast to the typical steam-powered trains of the early 1930s. Martin P. Blomberg (later known for his four- and six-axle locomotive truck designs) patented the shape of the new train, which included its distinctive front-end with mouth-like grille and three-car articulated arrangement. The train emulated contemporary aircraft construction and was made from riveted aluminum, previously unknown for train design. GM supplied a Winton distillate engine to power the train. Although a pioneer compact Winton 201 diesel was considered, it was still experiencing teething issues; the spark-plug-ignition distillate engine was a proven type and a design familiar to Fetters.

February 12, 1934 was a historic day as Union Pacific's sleek Pullman streamliner, M10000, made its debut. Compared to conventional heavyweight trains, the streamliner was compact with a low profile, riding just 9½ inches above the rails. The three-section articulated train (including power unit) weighed just 85 tons, about the same as a single heavyweight passenger car. The train could exceed 110 mph on level track—too fast for regular service, but great for publicity stunts. More significantly, the train could run 900 miles between fueling stops (and never had to stop for water), and had the ability to run for hundreds of miles at sustained high speed. It was inexpensive to operate compared with a steam-hauled train. The train's bright forward-facing headlight was augmented with a bright vertically aimed light to announce its approach while racing across the prairies.

The interior exuded modern design; the cars were dressed in shades of blue

New E2 diesels lead the re-equipped *City of Los Angeles* across the desert on this colorized postcard view on the Los Angeles & Salt Lake route in the late 1930s. The *COLA* was originally on a weekly schedule that augmented UP's other named trains between Chicago and Los Angeles. *Richard Jay Solomon collection*

The E2s were unique to the UP (together with its partners on the *COLA* and *COSF*). They were internally identical to EAs and E1s, but the E2 A units had bulbous noses unique to the model. Later Es adopted the standardized slanted nose. *Electro-Motive Corp.*

with a very light shade at the apex of the ceiling gradually darkening as it progressed downward. Aluminum stripes separated the various color shades and the window sills were black. Soft electric lighting could be adjusted to three basic levels of intensity, the lowest intended for overnight running. Venetian blinds covered the windows. Seating was two-by-two with neutral golden-brown upholstery. Seats were designed to comfortably recline with tray tables, similar to aircraft design, and likewise the windows featured UV-coated glass to protect passengers from exposure to direct sun.

The train was a gimmick, a slick public relations tool designed to capture the public imagination and show what the railroad was capable of achieving. Rather than simply press it into service, UP sent it on a 12,625-mile cross-country barnstorming

An A-B set of Fairbanks-Morse 2,000-hp Erie-built diesels and an Alco PB lead train No. 2, the eastbound *Los Angeles Limited* (Los Angeles-Chicago) east of Echo, Utah. *Union Pacific*

tour advertised as "Tomorrow's Train Today," making no fewer than 68 stops to allow for public inspections—including one by President Franklin D. Roosevelt. The streamliner's "15 minutes of fame" ended quickly: Although UP ordered a fleet of similar GM-powered Pullman trains, the M10000's short, inflexible consist made it unsuitable for high-volume, long-distance services, and it was assigned to a relatively obscure run as the *City of Salina* on the old Kansas Pacific from Kansas City to Salina, Kan. In 1942, after running 900,000 miles in service, the UP scrapped the M10000 at Omaha, with the railroad proudly donating its aluminum body for the American war effort. By contrast, Burlington's stainless-steel, diesel-powered *Zephyr*—which debuted two months after the M10000—served until the late 1950s, and is today preserved at Chicago's Museum of Science and Industry.

Union Pacific placed a fleet of similarly designed Pullman-built streamliners in regular revenue service on high-profile runs during the mid-1930s. The design of the later trains gradually evolved from the innovative M10000 into more functional trains pulled by conventional diesel locomotives. Articulated design gave way to more flexible conventionally coupled streamlined passenger cars, and the compact low-profile cars received more conventional styling, but still featured lightweight construction.

City of Portland

The concepts introduced with the three-car M10000 were expanded on the next train delivered. The similar-looking six-car train, designated M10001, was powered by the recently introduced 900-hp Winton 201A diesel engine. It was UP's first diesel-powered streamlined train and the country's first diesel-powered sleeping-car train, with articulated sleepers named *E.H. Harriman,*

CITY OF SAN FRANCISCO WRECK OF 1939

On the evening of Aug. 12, 1939, just weeks before Germany and Russia invaded Poland to ignite World War II in Europe, the *City of San Francisco* suffered one of the worst incidents of railroad sabotage in the U.S. during the 20th century. Near Harney, Nev., a suspected saboteur deliberately damaged main-line rails, removing joint bars and pulling sections of rail almost 5 inches out of alignment on the outside of a curve on the tracks approaching a bridge over the Humboldt River. The signaling system was also tampered with (Harriman-era lower-quadrant semaphores with track-circuit block protection that would have gone to red if the track circuit was broken). In the dark of night, with the signaling system showing a false clear, the ill-fated train derailed at the tampered section of track while traveling at 60 mph; several cars fell into the riverbed, resulting in 24 deaths. The FBI conducted a thorough investigation and the SP offered a $10,000 reward for information leading to arrests, but while SP's chief of police continued investigating for many years, the saboteur or saboteurs were never found. It was believed that the perpetrators had intimate knowledge railroad engineering and of this particular section of railroad, which made the incident especially chilling.

Opposite: Cars on *The Challenger* had brightly lit modern interior decor and amenities—such as an on-board nurse—that would appeal to women passengers traveling with children. Chair cars, such as this one, featured comfortable reclining seats with ample leg room.
Union Pacific

Abraham Lincoln, and *Oregon Trail.* Unlike the M10000, the M10001 was designed for long-haul service. Like the other pioneer streamliners, it made a publicity tour, including a cross-country dash on Oct. 22, 1934, from Los Angeles to New York City's Grand Central Terminal. This was accomplished in just 56 hours, 55 minutes, nearly a full day faster than the railroad's regularly scheduled steam-hauled passenger trains.

On May 5, 1935, the M10001 entered regular *City of Portland* service between Chicago and Portland, making it America's first regularly scheduled streamlined train to the West Coast. It made its 39½-hour, 2,272-mile run using C&NW between Chicago and Omaha, UP's Overland Route west to Granger, Wyo., and from there on the Oregon Short Line route to the Pacific Northwest. UP later upgraded the power car with a more-powerful 1,200-hp Winton diesel and added a diner-lounge to make it a seven-car train.

In June 1935, Union Pacific introduced additional Pullman articulated train sets featuring longer consists, which reflected the growing popularity of the streamliners. On May 15, 1936, the M10002 made its debut as the *City of Los Angeles.* This shared styling with the M10001 and M10000 but was powered by a pair of Winton diesel engines.

City of San Francisco

UP's most famous streamliner was the *City of San Francisco* (train Nos. 101 westbound and 102 eastbound), which made its debut on June 14, 1936. Operated jointly with C&NW and Southern Pacific, the M10004 was a Pullman-built nine-car lightweight articulated train with twin power cars to handle SP's Sierra Nevada grades. A backup power car set carried the number M10003. UP's later articulated streamlined power cars (M10003 through M10006) employed a different profile, taking styling cues from General Motors' automotive design. This included an elevated cab overlooking a long hood, with a front end grill resembling a fierce grin.

This lightweight train was soon found inappropriate for the Overland service, and in 1937 an improved train with larger-profile streamlined cars—led by custom-styled Electro-Motive E2 diesels—was introduced on the route. The train was jointly owned by the three Overland Route partners and the locomotive nose proudly displayed all

In the mid-1930s, UP aimed to attract passengers back to the railroad by offering innovative trains. In 1935 it introduced *The Challenger* (Chicago-Los Angeles) that would appeal to middle-class travelers by offering comfortable, fashionable accommodations with affordable fares.
Union Pacific

three company logos, with UP's on top. In its early years, the lone *City of San Francisco* was scheduled like premium steamship service and made just one round trip to Oakland every six days. The popularity of the train warranted more investment, and a second consist entered *COSF* service in 1941. The train was made daily in 1947 with the addition of yet more equipment, and it served as the Overland Route's flagship passenger train until the coming of Amtrak in 1971.

City of Denver

Union Pacific's final Pullman articulated streamliner was the *City of Denver*. The schedule was covered by two train sets, Nos. M10005 and M10006. The trains consisted of 12 to 14 Pullman cars. At the time of its inauguration, the *City of Denver* was advertised as the world's fastest train based on its Omaha to Denver sprint, which averaged just over 75 mph.

To maintain its various streamlined services, UP swapped train sets as required. For example, the M10002 set built for the *City of Los Angeles* filled in on the *City of Denver* and *City of Portland* runs in later years, while the original *City of San Francisco* set was reconfigured and reassigned to the *City of Los Angeles*.

By 1940, articulated trains had fallen out of favor because of their inherent operational limitations and capacity constraints. Also, by the late 1930s, Electro-Motive had advanced the designs of the early streamlined power cars into stand-alone diesel-electric locomotives. Pullman and other builders were introducing non-articulated streamlined lightweight cars that offered weight savings but allowed railroads to easily adjust the length of trains to match passenger counts. All of UP's groundbreaking articulated streamliners were scrapped by the early 1950s.

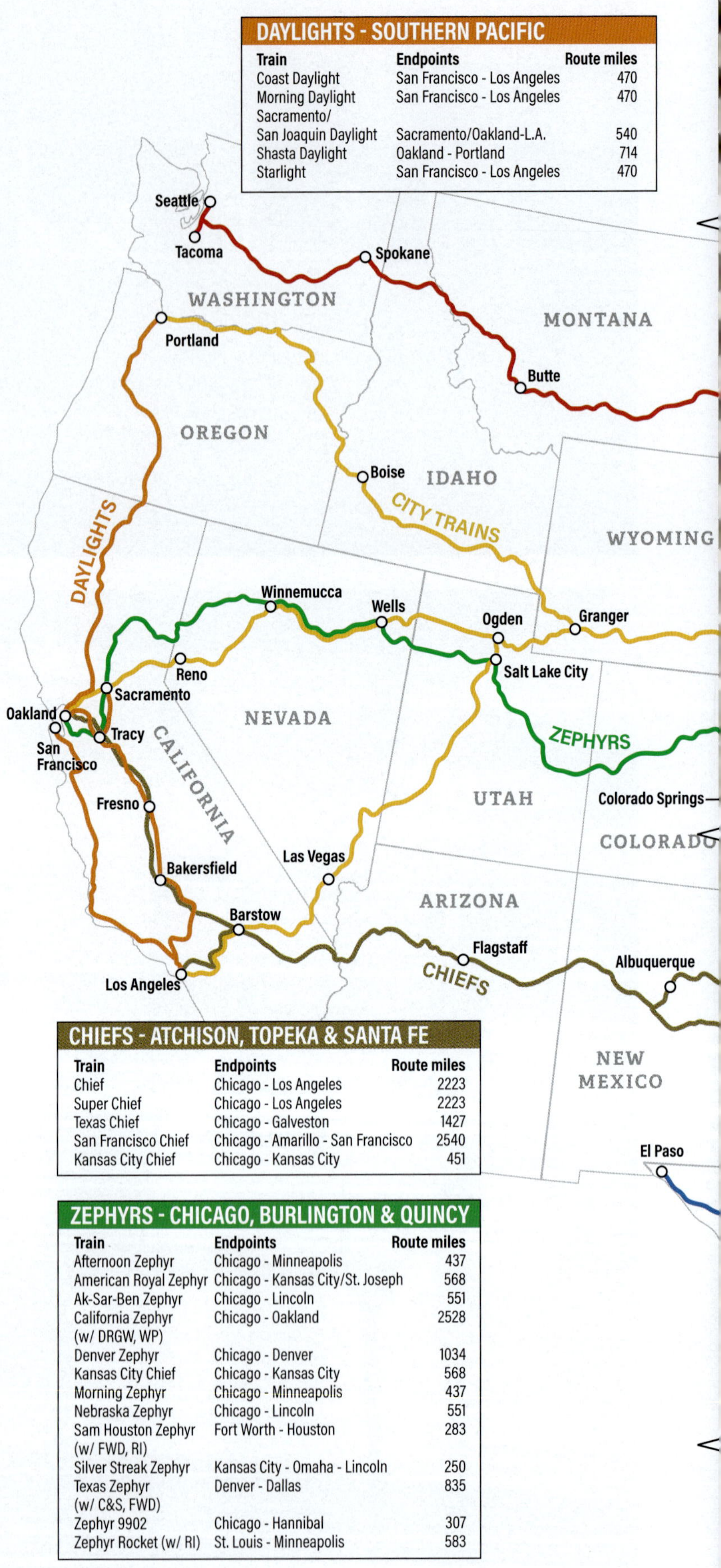

DAYLIGHTS - SOUTHERN PACIFIC

Train	Endpoints	Route miles
Coast Daylight	San Francisco - Los Angeles	470
Morning Daylight	San Francisco - Los Angeles	470
Sacramento/ San Joaquin Daylight	Sacramento/Oakland-L.A.	540
Shasta Daylight	Oakland - Portland	714
Starlight	San Francisco - Los Angeles	470

CHIEFS - ATCHISON, TOPEKA & SANTA FE

Train	Endpoints	Route miles
Chief	Chicago - Los Angeles	2223
Super Chief	Chicago - Los Angeles	2223
Texas Chief	Chicago - Galveston	1427
San Francisco Chief	Chicago - Amarillo - San Francisco	2540
Kansas City Chief	Chicago - Kansas City	451

ZEPHYRS - CHICAGO, BURLINGTON & QUINCY

Train	Endpoints	Route miles
Afternoon Zephyr	Chicago - Minneapolis	437
American Royal Zephyr	Chicago - Kansas City/St. Joseph	568
Ak-Sar-Ben Zephyr	Chicago - Lincoln	551
California Zephyr (w/ DRGW, WP)	Chicago - Oakland	2528
Denver Zephyr	Chicago - Denver	1034
Kansas City Chief	Chicago - Kansas City	568
Morning Zephyr	Chicago - Minneapolis	437
Nebraska Zephyr	Chicago - Lincoln	551
Sam Houston Zephyr (w/ FWD, RI)	Fort Worth - Houston	283
Silver Streak Zephyr	Kansas City - Omaha - Lincoln	250
Texas Zephyr (w/ C&S, FWD)	Denver - Dallas	835
Zephyr 9902	Chicago - Hannibal	307
Zephyr Rocket (w/ RI)	St. Louis - Minneapolis	583

Key Passenger Trains 1950-1970

Union Pacific and competing railroads (including future merger partners)

ROCKETS - ROCK ISLAND

Train	Endpoints	Route miles
Corn Belt Rocket	Chicago - Omaha	493
Choctaw Rocket	Memphis - Oklahoma City	486
Choctaw Rockette	Memphis - Amarillo	762
Des Moines Rocket	Chicago - Des Moines	358
Jet Rocket	Chicago - Peoria	161
Kansas City Rocket	Minneapolis - Fort Worth	1080
Oklahoma Rocket	Kansas City - Oklahoma City	407
Peoria Rocket	Chicago - Peoria	161
Quad City Rocket	Chicago - Rock Island	181
Rocky Mtn. Rocket	Chicago-Denver/Colorado Springs	1151
Texas Rocket	Minneapolis - Fort Worth	1080
Twin Star Rocket	Minneapolis - Houston	1363
Zephyr Rocket	Minneapolis - Burlington (CB&Q) - St. Louis	583

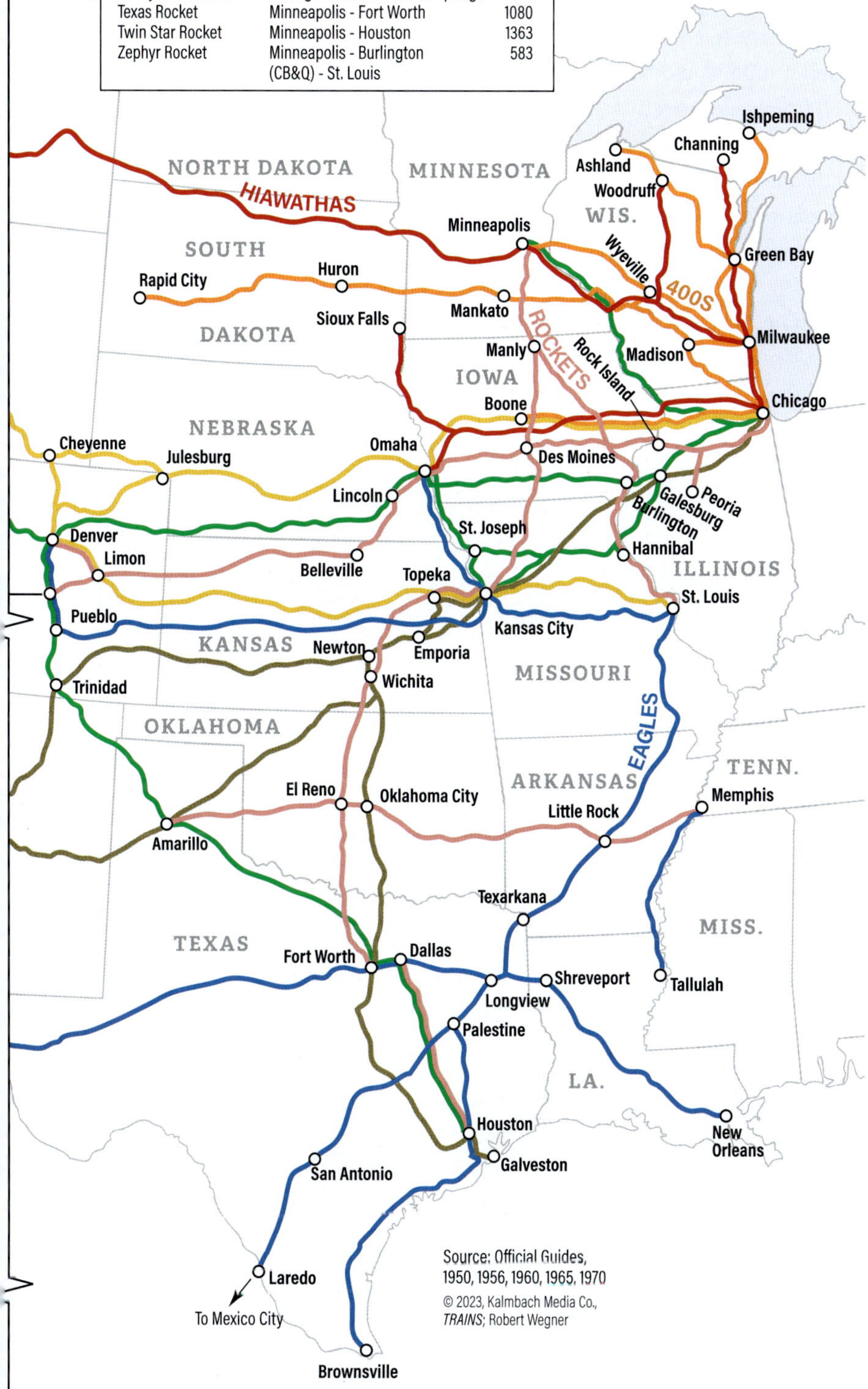

HIAWATHAS - MILWAUKEE ROAD

Train	Endpoints	Route miles
Afternoon Hiawatha	Chicago - Minneapolis	421
Chippewa Hiawatha	Chicago - Channing	315
Hiawatha (N. Woods)	New Lisbon - Woodruff	170
Midwest Hiawatha	Chicago - Omaha/Sioux Falls	604
Morning Hiawatha	Chicago - Minneapolis	421
Olympian Hiawatha	Chicago - Tacoma/Seattle	2227

400S - CHICAGO & NORTH WESTERN

Train	Endpoints	Route miles
Capitol 400	Chicago - Milwaukee - Madison	167
City of Milw. 400	Chicago - Milwaukee	85
Commuter 400	Chicago - Milwaukee	85
Dakota 400	Chicago - Huron - Rapid City	940
Flambeau 400	Chicago - Ashland	452
Green Bay 400	Chi. - Sheyboygan - Green Bay	213
Kate Shelley 400	Chicago - Boone	340
Minnesota 400	Wyeville - Mankato	191
Peninsula 400	Chicago - Ishpeming	392
Shoreland 400	Chicago - Green Bay	201
Streamliner 400	Chicago - Milwaukee	85
Twin Cities 400	Chicago - Minneapolis	419
Valley 400	Chicago - Appleton - Green Bay	213

CITY TRAINS - UNION PACIFIC

Train	Endpoints	Route miles
City of Denver	Chicago - Denver*	1048
City of Kansas City	K. C. - Denver - Cheyenne	746
City of Los Angeles	Chicago - Los Angeles*	2299
City of Las Vegas	Los Angeles - Las Vegas	335
City of Portland	Chicago - Portland*	2271
City of St. Louis (w/ WAB)	St. Louis - Cheyenne	1024
City of San Francisco (w/ SP)	Chicago - Oakland	2260

*Chicago - Omaha operated by Chicago & North Western until 1955, then Milwaukee Road

EAGLES - MISSOURI PACIFIC

Train	Endpoints	Route miles
Aztec Eagle (w/NdeM)	San Antonio - Mexico City	956
Colorado Eagle (w/ DRGW)	St. Louis - Denver	1021
Delta Eagle	Memphis - Tallulah	259
Louisiana Eagle (w/ T&P)	New Orleans - Fort Worth	547
Missouri River Eagle	St. Louis - K.C. - Omaha	478
Texas Eagle (w/ T&P)	St. Louis - El Paso	1378
Texas Eagle (w/ T&P)	St. L. - Houston/San Antonio	1075
Valley Eagle	Houston - Brownsville	371

Source: Official Guides, 1950, 1956, 1960, 1965, 1970

© 2023, Kalmbach Media Co., *TRAINS*; Robert Wegner

Challenger

In the mid-1930s, on the heels of the excitement spurred by its early streamliners, Union Pacific continued to seek innovative ways to improve its passenger trains. The railroad engaged a consultant to conduct market research to better understand what its passengers wanted from train travel. Among the lessons learned was that a large group of passengers disdained what they considered drab conventional Pullman sleeping cars and service. Union Pacific aimed to change this with an all-new Chicago-Los Angeles train. The *Challenger,* introduced in 1935, was named after UP's popular Sun Valley, Idaho, lodge. It was designed to attract middle-class travelers and offered basic amenities—but above the simple coach level—providing comfortable accommodation in the latest styles at an affordable fare.

Unlike the innovative M-series streamliners, the *Challenger* was a conventional steam-powered train, neither articulated nor diesel powered, but with new heavyweight sleeping car designs that featured upbeat, brightly lit interiors. A key to the train's success was improved on-board service: the crew was specially trained, female nurses served as stewardesses, and a car was assigned exclusively to female travelers in an effort to attract women

The *Challenger* was introduced with conventional equipment featuring redesigned interiors. It was the product of consultants that UP engaged to explore how to make rail travel more appealing. *Union Pacific*

In the mid-1950s, UP bought a fleet of American Car & Foundry Astra Domes to upgrade streamlined trains to "Domeliners," including the *City of Los Angeles,* shown here in a publicity photo at Glendale, Calif., near Los Angeles.
Union Pacific

traveling with children. The concept was a success, and soon UP introduced similar trains between Chicago-San Francisco (with C&NW and SP) and Chicago-Portland (with C&NW) in an effort to revitalize passenger traffic. The *San Francisco Challenger* was a conventional consist that began in 1936, equipped with air-conditioned luxury reclining-seat coaches.

A year later, on July 8, 1937, UP's *Forty Niner* made its debut. Named to honor the Gold Rush pioneers that helped settle California, this was a modern-looking train designed to help carry an expected swell of traffic for the Golden Gate Exposition held at Treasure Island in San Francisco in 1939. This steam-powered, streamlined, all-Pullman consist presented a notable contrast to the UP's diesel lightweight trains. It was a heavyweight, eight-car train with stylized streamlined gloss but lacking much of the advanced technology associated with the early streamlined trains. It was roller-bearing equipped, and the tail car was a streamlined articulated observation. Two steam locomotives, 4-6-2 Pacific No. 2906 and 4-8-2 Mountain No. 7002, were rebuilt by the Omaha shops with roller bearings and lightweight rods; they were also given a streamlined shroud and specially painted for the run. The train was discontinued in 1941 and its equipment reallocated.

To take pressure off other Overland trains, during the summer seasons of 1939 and 1940 UP operated the *Treasure*

UP ordered its first 15 Astra Domes from ACF in 1952, and ultimately bought 35 of the cars; the rest were delivered during 1954 and 1955. Among the features of the Astra Dome were seats angled toward windows. *Union Pacific*

Island Special on a weekly basis on the Overland route accommodating Exposition passengers. This was discontinued when the second weekly *City of San Francisco* was introduced.

Postwar streamliners

Following World War II, the UP invested heavily in diesel-electric locomotives and modern lightweight passenger cars to greatly expand its streamlined services. In 1946, UP and Wabash introduced the *City of St. Louis* to connect St. Louis, Kansas City, Denver and Cheyenne, Wyo. Originally this also carried a few through cars that were switched onto trains for Los Angeles, Oakland, and Portland. In 1951, UP assigned the *City of St. Louis* as a through run to Los Angeles. By late 1947, UP had enough streamlined equipment to operate the *City of Portland, City of Los Angeles,* and *City of San Francisco* on daily schedules. Additional cars also allowed for longer consists.

Toward the end of World War II, General Motors planned for development of glass-topped dome cars to give passengers panoramic views. This evolved into a concept train called the *Train of Tomorrow,* designed and built as a joint effort between various divisions of General Motors and Pullman-Standard. The train made its

Nothing could be finer than dinner in an Astra Dome diner. If this photo didn't convince you to book a ticket West on Union Pacific, nothing would.
Union Pacific

debut in May 1947 and consisted of low-profile dome cars hauled by a single smartly painted E7. It made a nationwide tour to promote modern passenger train design. In 1950, Union Pacific bought the *Train of Tomorrow* set and assigned it to the Portland-Seattle run.

Dome cars were among the most popular innovations of postwar streamlined train travel, and UP's competition—notably the Burlington—embraced domes on their sleekest trains. Union Pacific ordered 15 dome-lounge cars and 10 dome-diners built by American Car & Foundry in 1952, and later rostered more than 40 domes, including a handful of Pullman-built cars. They were largely assigned to the *City of Los Angeles, City of Portland, City of St. Louis,* and *Challengers*. The dome-diners were especially popular, as they offered some of the greatest railroad experiences in the West: passengers were delighted to enjoy a meal while racing along in a *City* streamliner.

General Motors *Aerotrain*

In the 1950s, the UP was among several railroads that expressed renewed interest in a new breed of innovative lightweight trains to attract passengers while lowering operating costs. UP briefly flirted with General Motors' *Aerotrain,* the latest in lightweight streamlined train design. Promotional

UNION

Later versions of the *City of Los Angeles* were dome-equipped. The UP staged this publicity photo of the train behind E8 No. 928 and a pair of B units in the 1950s. Note the train number in the locomotive's number boards. *Union Pacific*

On Jan. 22, 2002, spotless specially painted SD70M-2s Nos. 2002 and 2001 lead UP's Olympic Special train past Dougren, Ore., on the former Southern Pacific. The train is working uphill from Eugene, Ore., into the Cascades. This train ran over the system prior to the Salt Lake City Winter Olympics carrying the Olympic Flame in a special cauldron car. *Brian Jennison*

materials touted that the design melded highway and railway technology and that it could "revolutionize rail travel." GM's chief engineer, W.H. Harvey, explained in the December 1955 *Railway Age* that the train was named for its unique air-suspension system designed for two-axle cars (one axle at each end) to provide a more comfortable ride. A system of eight air bellows supported axles on each car, while sophisticated pressure regulation was employed keep the passenger car bodies level relative to the track.

The train was hauled by a GM Electro-Motive Division model LWT12, a custom-styled streamlined, lightweight diesel. It was semi-permanently connected to the *Aerotrain's* low-riding cars, which consisted of modified bus bodies riding on railroad wheels. Union Pacific briefly leased a lone *Aerotrain* set from General Motors, and from December 1956 until September 1957 assigned it to the new *City of Las Vegas* (Los Angeles-Las Vegas). Despite the innovative technology, the axle design didn't work as well as hoped; passengers complained about its rough riding characteristics and the railroad found it underpowered, as it needed a helper to surmount Cajon Pass. GM's *Aerotrains* finished their careers on the Rock Island in Chicago suburban service; UP continued the *City of Las Vegas* using conventional equipment until 1962.

Park trains

Union Pacific capitalized on the scenic splendor of the West, and the railroad was a key to development of national parks and monuments across its service area. It seasonally marketed train service to

Utah's Bryce Canyon as well as Zion and Yellowstone national parks. The railroad was also an early proponent of the ski trade, operating Sun Valley, one of the West's earliest ski resorts, which it developed in the mid-1930s to boost winter ridership and further promote the railroad.

The railroad's Utah Parks subsidiary arranged for tours of that state's famous attractions, among them the Cedar Breaks National Monument, where the railroad owned the Cedar Breaks Lodge. Prior to the development of paved highways, Union Pacific offered the most-effective way for many visitors to reach these sites. It offered special trains for vacationers over its Cedar City Branch to Cedar City, Utah, which served as the gateway to the various Utah Parks; motor coaches then brought visitors to their various destinations.

In the 1950s, the *City of St. Louis* carried cars from June to September from Los Angeles, and Salt Lake City to Cedar City. During the same period UP ran the *Yellowstone Special,* bringing cars from Salt Lake City to UP's West Yellowstone (Mont.) Station, with highway transport into the park.

Inspired by the Swiss ski trade, UP management developed the Sun Valley resort to promote growing interest in winter sports. The resort is located about 69 miles north of Shoshone, Idaho (at an elevation around 6,000 feet above sea level) and was reached via UP's Ketchum Branch; Ketchum (Idaho) Station was served by a variety of seasonal trains. Sun Valley was famous for excellent snow for skiing and a relatively temperate climate. The resort was eventually expanded into an all-weather vacation destination catering to both wealthy and middle-class vacationers with the Challenger Inn offering lodging.

Decline to Amtrak

Passenger train historians mark 1952 as a high point for Union Pacific operations in the streamlined era. Through clever marketing, continued service improvements, and faster, more frequent trains, Union Pacific succeeded in rescuing

Only on Union Pacific could you find passenger-service SDP35s with an E9B leading a mixed consist of passenger cars and freight. This eastbound is passing the Salina, Kan., station in 1970, just months before Amtrak took control of UP passenger operations. *Paul Roth*

Neon lights highlight Denver Union Station in October 1973. This station was a nexus of passenger services in Colorado and in its heyday was served by Burlington, Missouri Pacific, Rio Grande, Rock Island, and Union Pacific. *Mel Patrick*

its passenger service from the depths of the Depression-era lows. However, despite massive investment in modern streamlined equipment and improved schedules, by the mid-1950s ridership was again declining—and this time it couldn't be saved. Interstate highway construction and affordable commercial jet travel sped the decline dramatically through the 1960s.

A major change occurred in 1955 when Union Pacific abandoned its traditional Chicago connection arrangement with Chicago & North Western, citing poor track conditions on that line. The UP moved its trains to Milwaukee Road instead, and for the last 15 years of UP passenger service, its trains at Chicago originated and terminated at Union Station instead of North Western Station.

By the late 1950s, UP and other railroads were trimming schedules and combining trains to curtail passenger-revenue losses. After 1956, the *Challenger* and *City of Los Angeles* were combined during the off seasons. In 1962, the famous *Overland* was melded with the *City of San Francisco,* and the cutbacks continued through the 1960s as many other trains gradually disappeared. By 1969, all remaining *City* streamliners were combined into one big train from Chicago that observers called "the City of Everywhere." Other trains were reduced to less-than-daily operation.

Although it curtailed the number of passenger trains and options, unlike some railroads UP didn't allow the quality of its existing service to deteriorate. It continued to invest in new passenger equipment into

the early 1960s (including buying the last EMD E units ever built, in 1964). Until it conveyed its passenger service to Amtrak on May 1, 1971, the UP's passenger trains were well maintained and well run, and most of its principal routes retained at least some scheduled passenger service.

Today, very little of the original Union Pacific passenger network hosts Amtrak intercity trains. The famed Overland, Kansas Pacific, OSL, and LA&SL routes are largely freight only. By contrast, many former SP routes still host Amtrak services and share tracks with UP freights.

In the first few years of Amtrak, services on UP lines closely resembled UP's late-era trains. In November 1972, 18 months after Amtrak startup, westbound No. 5 departing Cheyenne, Wyo., meets a 6900-series DDA40X with an eastbound freight. *Mel Patrick*

CHAPTER 4

FREIGHT OPERATIONS

Union Pacific's key lines are among the nation's busiest freight routes

General Electric ES44AC (UP class C45ACCTE) No. 5325 leads a westbound double-stack train at the remote Sano siding on July 30, 2009. The siding is on the former Western Pacific, 36 miles west of Gerlach, Nev. *Brian Solomon*

Freight has long been Union Pacific's lifeblood and the primary source of revenue for the company. Rapid industrial growth of the West during World War II and the swell of population in the post-war years contributed to UP's role as a primary freight artery. In 1949, annual freight traffic exceeded 56 million tons (with freight revenues five times greater than that from passenger traffic) with the average haul of a freight train more than 560 miles.

This is UP's $3.5 million North Platte hump yard as it appeared when new in 1948. The view of the hump looks down toward the bowl tracks. Retarders automatically regulate the speed of freight cars rolling into the bowl. *Union Pacific*

Historically, agricultural products such as grain, perishables (fruit and vegetables), and livestock represented the largest portion of freight by tonnage. The primary focus of transcontinental traffic was on UP's east-west main line from eastern interchange partners through the Omaha/Council Bluffs gateway to Ogden, Utah, for interchange with Southern Pacific; with traffic to the Pacific Northwest via the Oregon Short Line; and Los Angeles traffic continuing westward via Salt Lake City over the Los Angeles & Salt Lake route.

Evolving traffic, combined with the emergence of intermodal transportation, the shift toward point-to-point unit trains for bulk traffic, and merger with other lines have produced numerous changes to the way UP moves freight and the role of yards on the network. In the 1970s, prior to the expansion of its routes through merger, UP established itself as a major bulk carrier, hosting a large number of unit trains transporting commodities from coal and grain to soda ash and aggregates.

In 1994, prior to merging Chicago & North Western and Southern Pacific, UP's heaviest traffic in terms of annual tonnage was on its Nebraska trunk between Gibbon and O'Fallons. Gibbon Junction is where the Marysville Subdivision diverged, carrying traffic eastward toward important gateways at Kansas City, St. Louis, and beyond.

North Platte Yard has long been the busiest on the UP system. This view shows how the retarder hump appeared when it was new in 1948. *Union Pacific*

O'Fallons is the junction a few miles west of North Platte that from 1984 onward gained importance as the route to the Powder River basin, a huge source of new traffic moving eastward over the railroad. The growth of coal traffic contributed to a preponderance of eastbound tonnage from east of O'Fallons to Gibbon Junction, with greater tonnage routed eastward over the Marysville Subdivision and then continuing on the main line toward Omaha. This was the exception to a general preponderance of westward tonnage over most of the traditional Union Pacific.

Traffic to the Pacific Northwest represented about half the railroad's tonnage west of Cheyenne, Wyo., with roughly an equal split between traffic moving over the former Western Pacific and SP's route to northern California, and traffic moving via the LA&SL to southern California.

Former Missouri Pacific routes also accommodated significant traffic. From Chicago, traffic followed the former Chicago & Eastern Indiana routes southwest toward and around St. Louis and southward to North Little Rock, Ark.—a major focal point for traffic in the southeastern part of UP's network. Memphis, Tenn., gateway traffic came in from the east, while additional traffic headed southeast to eastern Louisiana (including New Orleans) and south/southwest to northern Louisiana, Oklahoma, Texas, the Mexican border, and northwest toward Kansas City.

The merger with C&NW solidified UP's traffic between Council Bluffs and Chicago, while the merger with SP re-established Overland Route traffic over the old Central Pacific route. It also provided UP with several other important corridors, notably the vital crossing of the Tehachapis; the busy Sunset Route (LA to New Orleans) and Golden State Route (LA via El Paso to Kansas City and Chicago) that were key to expansion of transcontinental intermodal business; former Rio Grande routes in Colorado and Utah that offered access to low-sulphur coal traffic; and former Cotton Belt lines across Texas, Louisiana, and Arkansas.

Since the early 20th century, UP has operated some of America's most powerful locomotives to haul exceptionally long freights. In the mid-1990s, the advent

of AC traction diesels and perfection of distributed power technology has enabled the railroad to run heavier trains than ever before. As trains grew much longer and heavier, the railroad needed longer sidings, more main tracks, and in some places larger yards, especially for intermodal traffic. Improvements to main routes have included reducing curvature and grades through line relocations and construction of low-grade cutoffs, as well as improvements to increase clearances and weight limits to allow taller and heavier trains. Advances in traditional signaling have improved safety, increased line capacity, and lowered operating costs, while advances in computer technology and improved communications enabled consolidation of dispatching centers.

Union Pacific's hump classification yard at Pocatello, Idaho was built in the late 1940s to accommodate growing traffic after World War II. This view shows the hump towers, with retarders to slow the descent of cars into bowl tracks. Left of the classification yard is a long train of PFE reefers. *Trains collection*

Yards

As Union Pacific freight business blossomed, its yards grew in size to accommodate the swell of traffic. Since the 1960s, the shift from traditional carload traffic to intermodal trains and long single-commodity and unit trains have reduced the comparative volume of cars requiring mid-journey classification. UP and SP were once major conduits for perishable traffic and livestock moves, but as this traffic declined, the facilities once used to classify and service perishable traffic were scaled back and abandoned or reallocated for other purposes.

In recent decades Union Pacific has made a large investment in intermodal terminals and transfer points, while development of Powder River coal traffic and the growth of Gulf Coast petrochemical traffic required new specialized facilities. The UP and its predecessors operated some of the largest and best-known classification yards in the West. In addition to these expansive miles-long seas of track and cars are numerous smaller yards.

In recent years, continued decline of carload traffic led to closure or downsizing

On July 29, 1984, a Missouri Pacific freight rolls west through Mill Creek Valley as seen from the Compton Avenue overpass in St. Louis. Since that time, most of the tracks in this scene have been removed; all that remain are two UP tracks, three for Terminal Railroad Association, and two for Metrolink's light-rail line. *Scott Muskopf*

of many traditional classification yards. UP's system-wide reorganization, called Unified Plan 2020 (announced in 2018), implemented Precision Scheduled Railroading strategies, which included shifting the focus to flat switching yards from gravity hump yards where traffic volumes were below a predetermined threshold. This resulted in many changes to large yards across the network.

Bailey Yard (North Platte)

The most significant yard on the network is the sprawling Bailey Yard at North Platte, Neb., 281 timetable miles west of Omaha. It is the largest, most-important yard on the UP system, spawned during the railroad's massive post-World War II investment. The original five-mile-long North Platte hump opened in November 1948. It was improved during the 1950s with a state-of-the-art computer controlled hump-classification system. Computer-regulated retarders allowed UP to significantly expand hump capacity while minimizing incidents of hard coupling—events that tended to damage freight cars and their lading. The retarders were innovative when installed, using infrared sensors to accurately gauge the speed of cars descending the hump.

In 1968, the North Platte facility was renamed Bailey Yard for former UP president Edd H. Bailey. This followed expansive improvements that transformed the facility, including a new second hump dedicated to classification for eastbound

traffic, with the original hump assigned to westbound classification. In 1980, UP replaced the original hump with a 50-track westbound classification yard.

Strategically situated in the "waist of the hourglass," Bailey Yard is at the operational center of the traditional UP system, making it an ideal place to classify traffic destined across the network. To the west of North Platte the UP faces heavy grades; to the East it is relatively level. As Powder River coal business blossomed in the 1980s and 1990s, the railroad built a built a large coal yard at North Platte that could hold up to 450 coal cars on seven tracks.

Bailey's vast size, combined with its intense rail activity, has made it a local tourist attraction, and the railroad has built a small visitors' center on the south side of the yard near the locomotive shops. By 2000, Bailey covered 2,850 acres, stretched along 8 miles of main line, and processed an average of 10,000 cars daily. The twin humps account for 114 tracks, while the yard had 315 miles of track. At its peak during the coal boom of the late 1990s and early 2000s, Union Pacific operated upward of 135 freight trains daily through North Platte, with about half of these eastbound unit coal trains or empties returning west. In recent years softening coal traffic and the adoption of Precision Scheduled Railroading (which encourages operation of fewer and longer freights) has resulted in fewer mainline movements through North Platte and elsewhere around the system.

In 1970, UP filmed its original "Great Big Rollin' Railroad" 60-second television ad at Bailey Yard. This featured a catchy song by Bill Fries (later of C.W. McCall fame) sung by the yard's employees with images of trains and freight cars rolling along. (Look it up on YouTube—it's worth the view!)

California yards

Prior to mergers with Western Pacific and Southern Pacific, UP's California traffic was largely focused in greater Los Angeles where East Yard was the primary gathering point for freight. Built during 1924-1925, in the steam era, East Yard consisted of a 1,000-car receiving yard, a 700-car eastbound classification yard, and an 880-car westbound classification yard, plus support facilities and a major locomotive shop. In the 1970s, UP improved it by adding a 16-track hump yard. As UP's intermodal traffic grew, the railroad expanded East Yard as an intermodal terminal, and in 1990 UP closed the hump. A nearby secondary yard, known as Weeds Yard, served local industries, while various other small LA-area yards supported UP's area carload traffic.

Working the east end of Southern Pacific's Roseville (Calif.) Yard, a pair of venerable SP SD7s catch the evening sun after clouds cleared following a day of heavy rain in February 1990. Since UP assumed operation of SP in 1996, it invested millions to upgrade the yard.
Brian Solomon

During 1980 and 1981, Union Pacific built a modern classification yard in the Mojave Desert at Yermo, Calif., with capacity for 1,500 cars. It was designed in part to assume carload classification previously focused on East Yard. By the mid-1990s, Yermo had an eight-track receiving/departure yard, a 19-track flat switching classification yard, and support facilities.

During most of the 1900s, Southern Pacific was the dominant railroad in Los Angeles, operating various yards in the Los Angeles area. In the late 1940s, it built Taylor Yard north of downtown Los Angeles. This large, state-of-the-art facility included a hump classification yard with a 2,900-car capacity and flat switching yards to handle another 4,400 cars. Traffic growth in Los Angeles in following decades strained Taylor. Espee looked to improve its area operations in the 1960s with its Palmdale Cutoff, which accommodated growing traffic over the Tehachapis. Where the new cutoff intersected the Sunset Route at West Colton, SP built an enormous modern classification yard that opened in 1973. The rise of West Colton Yard, combined with the decline of the Coast Line, enabled SP to scale back operations at Taylor and ultimately close the yard in 1985.

By the early 1990s, West Colton was emblematic of Sunset Route capacity constraints that complicated operations in SP's final years. Although relatively new, the sprawling yard proved inadequate for modern train lengths—it was ill-suited for the gigantic freights being run in the early 1990s. Congestion was further exacerbated by inadequate infrastructure for the volume of business heading to and from the Los Angeles and Long Beach port facilities. Complicating operations was the grade-level crossing with Santa Fe just east of the yard, which hosted UP's LA&SL route as well as Santa Fe's transcontinental traffic.

Among the improvements UP made to West Colton following the UP-SP merger was construction of the Colton Crossing Grade Separation. Planning began in

All across its system Union Pacific maintains yards to gather, store, classify, and assemble freight cars into trains. This 1950s view shows UP yards in Denver. *Trains collection*

In November 1972, GE U50C No. 5012 leads Rock Island GEs eastbound at Overton, Neb. The train is taking the center siding from the No. 1 track. The UP maintains center sidings at strategic locations that allow trains to clear main tracks to help keep the railroad fluid. Located just over 50 miles east of North Platte, the center siding at Overton had a 68-car capacity. *Mel Patrick*

2006, while the construction to elevate UP's former SP line over BNSF's line was undertaken between 2011 and 2013. This, along with other new infrastructure, greatly eased the flow of freight through the Los Angeles area.

In northern California, the most strategically important former SP yard is Roseville. It's located east of Sacramento, Calif., near the junction of the historic Shasta Route (now UP's Interstate 5 Corridor Valley Subdivision) and the Roseville Subdivision (the historic Overland Route over Donner Pass). In the steam era, Roseville consisted of four flat switching yards that assembled trains for movement over Donner Pass and reclassified inbound traffic from both the Shasta and Overland routes for various points in California. Pacific Fruit Express operated a large facility at Roseville that served as a hub for perishable train movements, and in the days before mechanical refrigerator cars, Roseville hosted the largest car icing facility in the world. SP invested heavily in upgrades at Roseville during the 1950s,

including a modern computerized double hump with 49 classification tracks. The humps were arranged to handle 3,750 cars a day during peak times, but allowed shutting down half of the hump during quiet periods.

Union Pacific invested heavily in Roseville after the merger with SP, rebuilding the yard between 1997 and 1999 and renaming the facility for former President and Chief Operating Officer Jerry R. Davis. The railroad boasts that this modern yard—six-miles long and covering 950 acres—is the largest yard west of the Rockies.

Texas yards

Texas is a major gathering area for carload traffic and an important intermodal destination and origin. The growth of the petrochemical industry and Gulf Coast port traffic have helped fuel impressive growth in carload business. Dozens of yards, from vast hump-classification yards processing thousands of cars daily to smaller regional staging yards are integral for UP in sorting traffic across the Lone Star state.

Greater Houston is a significant and growing source of traffic for UP. During

ABF

Viewed from atop Tunnel No. 10, Union Pacific priority symbol freight ZBRLC 10 is led by the Southern Pacific heritage unit on April 1, 2007. The train is spiraling through the famed Tehachapi Loop on the former SP at Walong, near Woodford, Calif.
Chris Guss

Missouri-Kansas-Texas GP7 No. 104 leads six other units past the Eureka Yard office in Houston on Jan. 10, 1988. This freight, known as "The Salty," is returning from Galveston Island with empty grain hoppers that had delivered loads of Midwestern wheat for transloading to ships docked at Galveston. *Tom Kline*

merger studies with SP, UP anticipated changes including restructuring SP's Englewood Yard for east-west traffic and UP's Settegast Yard for north-south traffic. The modern Englewood facility has its origins as the primary gathering and classification yard for SP Sunset Route freight traffic to and from Texas and Louisiana. In an early configuration, Englewood had a 48-track computerized hump with two massive receiving yards; expansions by the time of the UP-SP merger had increased the yard to 23 receiving tracks, 13 departure tracks, a 64-track classification yard, plus tracks for local traffic and an intermodal terminal. In a major reconstruction between 2020 and 2022, UP transformed Englewood into one of the railroad's premier facilities, doubling its hump capacity by lengthening the bowl tracks. It can now process up to 3,000 cars daily.

Houston's second-largest yard is Settegast, a former Missouri Pacific facility. In 1996, it included a six-track receiving yard, a six-track departure yard, and a 38-track hump classification yard that could process up to 1,750 cars daily, plus a large intermodal yard that performed about 117,000 lifts in 1994.

The Dallas-Fort Worth metroplex hosts several yards. The largest is Centennial Yard, a major hump yard serving the Fort Worth-El Paso main line. In 1996, it consisted of a 21-track receiving/departure yard and a 44-track classification yard; its daily capacity was 1,650 cars. Ney Yard, located south of downtown Fort Worth, is a smaller yard used for cross-border traffic with Mexico. It served as a holding yard while border documentation was collected. Davidson Yard (formerly Lancaster Yard), renamed in 2007 for former CEO Dick Davidson, was built on the site of a former Texas & Pacific yard that dated to the early 20th century. It was later developed to include a major diesel shop.

One of the railroad's newest large yards is Brazos in Robertson County, Texas, between Dallas and Houston. Construction began in 2018. It is near the site of the former SP Hearne Yard, which was at the junction and division point where traffic was classified for the Rio Grande Valley. The yard is designed to classify 1,300 cars daily.

UP's Global IV intermodal terminal is located in the far southwest side of Chicago near Joliet. Opened in 2010, the 550-acre facility handles more lifts than any other UP intermodal ramp in Chicago. Access from the north is via UP's Joliet Subdivision while the south end connects to BNSF's Chillicothe Subdivision to access trackage rights west to Kansas City. *Chris Guss*

The UP's former Missouri Pacific main line across Kansas and Colorado carried heavy Southern Pacific traffic through the mid-1990s. It was cut as a through route less than a year after the UP-SP merger. Near Bison, Kan., on Nov. 10, 1996, SD9043MAC No. 8063 leads westbound ASRVM-09 from East St. Louis, Ill. to Roseville, Calif. *Mike Abalos*

Proviso Yard (Chicago)

In 1903, Chicago & North Western built a modest yard in suburban Chicago at Melrose Park named Proviso Yard. As traffic volume grew, the C&NW greatly expanded the facility, and by 1930 it claimed the title of world's largest freight yard. For decades Proviso served as C&NW's most-important yard. After C&NW was acquired by UP in 1995, Proviso's 66-track hump served as UP's primary Chicago-area freight classification yard and a key sorting point for carload interchange freight.

In 2013, Proviso processed 18 to 24 inbound and outbound trains daily, with hump movements still manually controlled by retarder operators. As late as 2018, the yard was handling more than 2,600 cars on peak days. However, declining carload traffic and the yard's obsolete design caught up with it, and in July 2019, as part of Unified Plan 2020, UP closed Proviso's hump and shifted its work to North Platte's Bailey Yard.

Among the supplemental Chicago yards is West Chicago, where a smaller C&NW yard served as an automotive terminal and as a sorting yard for local traffic.

Kansas City yards

In 1950, Missouri Pacific began building a new state-of-the-art hump yard with computer-controlled retarders in Kansas City, Mo. Named for MP president Paul J. Neff, it consisted of East Yard (opened in 1955) and West Yard (opened in 1959). Neff Yard's 220 acres made it the largest on the MP system. It was designed for efficient movement of carload traffic and greatly improved the fluidity of cars passing though the Kansas City gateway by reducing the amount of car handling and cutting transit time.

Following the MP-UP merger, UP traffic moving through Kansas City increased significantly—by the mid-1980s, UP interchanged approximately 2,500 cars daily at KC. Neff's historic track arrangement was ill-suited for this traffic, so to improve traffic flow and streamline operations, UP conducted a thorough study of its Kansas City facilities. Neff Yard was the focus of multimillion dollar improvements that began in 1986. In April 1985, in conjunction with planned yard improvements, UP began construction of the Big Blue Hi-Line. This elevated 1½-mile cutoff spans the former MP north-south lines and tracks of Kansas City Southern on a 1,370-foot bridge as part of a signaled, grade-separated mainline (east-west) link through the Kansas City terminal area.

Armourdale was Southern Pacific's Kansas City facility, and it comprised two yards: West End Yard and Trainyard. As of 1995, West End featured a 21-track classification yard that processed westbound traffic from Chicago and St Louis. Trainyard sorted traffic for local destinations and interchange at Kansas City and also classified eastbound traffic that had not been pre-blocked. In its SP merger plan, UP anticipated consolidating Armourdale's functions at its other Kansas City yards, but this took years longer than expected.

Under Unified Plan 2000, UP closed the Neff Hump in October 2019 and a few months later shuttered Armourdale Yard, reassigning some classification functions to UP's nearby 18th Street Yard.

Louisiana and Arkansas

Immediately prior to merger with UP, MoPac had planned a new yard and acquired a 555-acre site along its Texas & Pacific main line 115 miles west of New Orleans. The site remained dormant for a decade before UP built Livonia Yard, which opened in May 1994. Built to serve the flourishing chemical business in Louisiana and east Texas, Livonia became UP's primary Louisiana freight hub. Livonia features a ten-track receiving/departure yard that supports a 25-track hump classification yard and processes about 1,350 cars daily. During 1994 and 1995, UP transferred the functions of Addis Yard in Baton Rouge, La., and Avon Yard in New Orleans to

Extra 71 West, led by a pair of double-engine DD35As, passes Lenwood on the Santa Fe west of Barstow, Calif., on March 31, 1979. *Brian Jennison*

Katy GP40 slug-mothers 227 and 226 bracket road slug No. 501 on Train 182 past Hennessey, west of Houston, on Feb. 15, 1988. Four covered hopper loads for cement-producer Texas Industries (TXI) in Katy, Texas, ride the front of the trailing consist while the rest of the train is empty Ortner rock hoppers headed back to the quarries near Georgetown in central Texas. *Tom Kline*

Livonia, which classified traffic for Texas and Arkansas points and also pre-blocked gateway traffic moving via New Orleans on connections via Norfolk Southern and CSX.

In 2021, UP lines in Louisiana originated more than 219,000 carloads and terminated almost 63,000, largely plastic pellets, industrial chemicals, and petroleum products. UP has several yards in Shreveport, La., notably Hollywood Yard, which historically supports interchange with both SP and Kansas City Southern and serves local industries, and Reisor Yard, which processes automotive traffic. SP also operated a small classification yard, with a separate facility for intermodal services.

In Arkansas, North Little Rock Yard was the second-largest classification yard on Missouri Pacific and was strategically situated near the confluence of four routes. The main line to St. Louis runs northward (also handling traffic to and from Memphis), while lines to Coffeyville, Kan., Texarkana, and Pine Bluff, Ark., diverged at junctions west of the yard. Part of the yard complex was MP's Downing B. Jenks Shops.

The UP invested in these important facilities, spending an estimated $13 million to upgrade the infrastructure between 1984 and 1986. A decade later, at the time of the UP-SP merger, the North Little Rock hump yard consisted of an 18-track receiving/departure yard and 64-track classification yard supported by 8- and 14-track yards for local traffic. The hump can classify 2,400 cars daily. As of 2021, North Little

The second section of Camas Prairie's Grangeville Turn eases onto the Halfmoon Trestle in Idaho's Lapwai Creek canyon on Sept. 17, 1994. This multiple-span wooden structure is 684-feet long and 141-feet tall. This was a joint BN/UP operation that ran with UP locomotives and a BN caboose. The train is returning from Grangeville to Lewiston, Idaho, working grades as steep as 3%. *Thomas L. Carver*

Rock was UP's second-largest carload classification yard, and Jenks is one of the most important diesel shops on the railroad.

The Cotton Belt operated a large hump classification yard at Pine Bluff, Ark., with a 14-track receiving/departure yard and a 42-track classification yard with capacity of 1,800 cars daily. Pine Bluff was also a primary Cotton Belt locomotive shop; UP used the facility until closing it in 2019.

Pacific Northwest

Following World War II, UP built its massive new Hinkle Yard near Hermiston, Ore., to replace older yards in the area that were displaced as result of line relocations necessitated by construction of dams along the Columbia River. Situated west of the Blue Mountains, Hinkle was fully operational by 1951. In 1978, UP improved the facility with a state-of-the-art hump designed to classify traffic generated in western Oregon and Washington. Union Pacific further renovated Hinkle between 1996 and 1998, including expansion of the locomotive shop to service up to 90 diesels daily. UP shuttered the Hinkle hump in 2019.

Portland is UP's largest Northwest terminal, where it operates several facilities including Albina and Barnes yards. On the eve of the SP merger, Albina sorted an average of 1,200 cars daily with a five-track receiving and departure yard, a 24-car classification yard, and a seven-track local facility. Barnes Yard is a 22-track waterfront facility serving industries around the port area

and includes two large grain elevators and an auto unloading facility. Smaller facilities around Portland included Bonneville, Kenton, and Rivergate yards. The UP also inherited SP's Brooklyn Yard, which had historically been a carload yard; in the years before the merger it was transformed by SP into an intermodal facility.

Union Pacific once maintained a significant hump classification yard at Pocatello, Idaho, strategically situated where the Pocatello Subdivision running west from Granger toward Portland intersects routes running north toward Butte, Mont., and south toward Ogden. The hump dated to the late 1940s and was built to handle the post-World War II traffic swell. To construct this largely new yard, UP relocated the Portneuf River. It had a 28-track classification yard, 14-track receiving yard with tracks up to 6,350-feet long, and an 11-track departure yard. In the early 1950s, it processed up to 2,200 cars daily, and served as gathering hub for perishable traffic. A double-track bypass was built to minimize delays to passenger trains, and it was later used by through freights as well. Changes in Northwest traffic patterns gradually quieted Pocatello, and in 2002 UP closed the yard in favor of other flat switching yards.

Intermodal traffic and terminals

Since the 1950s, intermodal traffic has had ever-increasing importance to Union

A southbound Union Pacific coal train from the Powder River Basin on the former Katy catches the last light of the day on Jan. 19, 2017. It's meeting a northbound empty train at the south switch at Mingo siding near Denton, Texas. The rolling track profile follows the uneven land in north Texas.
T.S. Hoover

Pacific, first with piggyback trailers and then shipping containers. Among the most significant changes resulted from UP's involvement handling Asian imports, the advent of double-stack container trains, and the effects of the 1980 Staggers Act that contributed to rapid growth of intermodal business.

In the 1960s, American involvement in Vietnam helped develop Asian trade corridors when the ships and containers delivering military supplies were engaged to backhaul goods from Japan and other Asian nations. Steamship companies were recognizing the economies of containerization, and by the early 1970s, UP's transcon competitors—notably Santa Fe and Burlington Northern—benefited from landbridge container service between West Coast ports and eastern U.S. markets. Staggers-era deregulation encouraged innovation, and allowed railroads to react more quickly to market changes. Southern Pacific began pioneering stack train operations in 1981 on its busy Sunset Route, and the concept quickly caught on with shipping companies, railroads, and car manufacturers.

In April 1984, Union Pacific and Chicago & North Western struck a deal with American President Lines to haul its containers from west coast ports to Chicago. This followed the established routing of UP-C&NW's jointly operated Falcon piggyback intermodal service. C&NW transformed its old Wood Street Yard in Chicago into an intermodal container terminal (later the site of C&NW's Global I intermodal terminal). Not long after UP-C&NW's stack train service began, APL extended its service eastward from Chicago over Conrail to reach New Jersey terminals. APL's LinerTrain container service cut two weeks from East Coast-bound containers from Asia compared to steamships via the Panama Canal.

The benefits of stack trains took hold, and in just few years trains of double-stacked containers went from a once-per-week novelty to a continuous parade of traffic. As stack traffic blossomed in 1990s and 2000s, it surpassed conventional piggyback and single-level container-on-flatcar service for most intermodal shipments. Most remaining piggyback (trailer) services are operated on request of high-volume intermodal shippers such as UPS.

As of 2022, former C&NW, MP, SP, and WP main lines remain key routes in UP's intermodal network, and the modern UP has more than 30 intermodal terminals in 24 major metropolitan areas and regional hubs. Major centers such as

Chicago, Los Angeles, and St. Louis feature multiple intermodal terminals.

Chicago intermodal

Greater Chicago is one of UP's most complex hubs, as it hosts five intermodal terminals. Global I is the former C&NW facility situated on UP's short Rockwell Subdivision. This accommodated four to six trains daily in 2014. More significant is the expansive Global II terminal that opened in 1990 adjacent to UP's massive Proviso Yard. This yard originates and terminates up to eight through trains daily. In addition to loading and unloading boxes (containers), it also handles traffic loaded at other Chicago-area facilities.

Global III is located in the cornfields west of Rochelle, Ill., about 75 miles west of downtown Chicago. It opened in 2003 with a capacity for 1,200 lifts daily, but was phased out in summer 2019 as a result of Unified Plan 2020. The facility has since been used primarily for block-swapping changes to operational patterns. Domestic traffic previously handled at Global III was shifted to Global II, while international traffic was shifted to Global IV, a modern intermodal ramp near Joliet that opened in 2010. Global IV allowed UP to phase out its former Missouri Pacific facilities at Canal Street south of downtown. UP's Yard Center intermodal facility is situated near the busy Dolton interlocking. Also a former MP yard, it handles traffic to and from the former Chicago & Eastern Illinois and traffic between the Chicago area and Texas and Mexico.

Los Angeles intermodal

Union Pacific operates several intermodal terminals across the greater Los Angeles area. The port facilities at Los Angeles/Long Beach are the busiest in the U.S., generating considerable traffic for Union Pacific. Port traffic grew rapidly during

UP Trains per Day: 2001

© 2023, Kalmbach Media Co., *TRAINS*; Terri Field

SD70ACe No. 8771 leads a westbound freight through downtown St. Louis on March 26, 2016. The venerable Union Station trainshed is visible to the left, just above the Interstate 64 viaduct. The disused Terminal Railroad Association Tower No. 1 can be seen in the distance near an eastbound UP coal train rolling along the TRRA line. *Scott Muskopf*

the 1980s and 1990s, but the poor state of the railway infrastructure limited the port's growth. In the late 1980s, regional authorities, port facilities, and the railroads involved worked to design a largely new intermodal route directly to the ports. The Alameda Corridor is the product of a public-private project including a new 20-mile grade-separated railroad—including a 10-mile-long, 40-foot-deep concrete trench—that connects the ports with the city of Los Angeles. The corridor opened in April 2002 at a cost of $2.4 billion. Served by BNSF and UP, the new line was handling more than 17,300 trains annually by 2005.

In May 2021, UP began work on its new Inland Empire Intermodal Terminal, located in a growing area east of Los Angeles populated by regional distribution centers. This is expected to serve domestic traffic moving to and through Chicago and Texas. Inland opened in late 2021 and is among UP's terminals operating 24 hours a day, seven days a week.

Powder River coal

Burlington Northern had developed the Powder River Basin in the 1970s to tap vast remote reserves of desirable low-sulfur subbituminous coal. In 1980, Chicago & North Western, with UP's help, put the logistical and legal machinery in motion to gain entry into the coal-rich Powder River Basin. The BN initially resisted competition, but in a high-profile ICC case, the regulatory agency reviewed C&NW's demand for access and required BN to relent. In 1983 BN and C&NW worked out a joint ownership agreement involving 93 miles of the newly constructed Orin Cutoff, which provided C&NW access to many of the mines in the region. However, to make use of this trackage, C&NW needed to extend its reach west.

Initially, C&NW had considered rebuilding more than 500 miles of its tired, low-traffic trans-Nebraska "Cowboy Line," which virtually intersected the Orin Line. Ultimately, this lightly built route was deemed inadequate to accommodate heavy unit trains. Since it would have been prohibitively expensive to upgrade the whole line, the C&NW's Western Railroad Properties subsidiary instead surveyed and built an all-new 56-mile line from a connection with UP at Joyce, Neb., to its Cowboy Line at Crandall. It invested in upgrading the portion of the Cowboy Line between Crandall and Shawnee, Wyo., and from there built another six miles of new line to reach shared trackage with BN (known as the Orin Cutoff) to reach Powder River mines.

Eastward from Joyce, C&NW coal trains rolled along Union Pacific rails, reaching the Nebraska main line at O'Fallons, where most coal continued east. Since UP's transcon traffic was already interchanged to C&NW east of the Missouri River Valley, this was the natural routing for coal flowing toward Chicago and beyond.

To service its unit trains and serve as a base of Powder River operations, C&NW built a coal terminal on the Orin Line at Bill, Wyo., and another on the Union Pacific east of Joyce at South Morrill, Neb. The North Western's first Powder River coal train moved eastward in 1984. Traffic mushroomed, and by the end of 1984 C&NW was operating about 11 unit trains daily out of the Basin.

Amendments to the Clean Air Act during the 1990s placed greater restrictions on sulfur dioxide emissions, resulting in a wide-scale switch toward low-sulfur Powder River coal. This contributed to a dramatic increase in traffic. To accommodate the greater volume, the railroads invested in more track capacity on the Orin Cutoff and connecting lines, including a second main track with bi-directional signaling. To keep pace with continued growth, UP and BNSF added sections of multiple main tracks in the boom years of the early 2000s. By 2007, approximately 39 miles of third main track served the Orin cutoff between Donkey Creek Junction and Shawnee Junction, with 14 miles of fourth main track over Logan Hill on the central portion of the Orin Line. The improvements were designed to enable moving 400 million tons of coal annually. On May 1, 2006, BNSF and Union Pacific together set a record by loading 76 Powder River coal trains in one day; by the end of that year the Orin Cutoff was considered the heaviest-tonnage line in the world.

However, since those boom times, changes in coal-burning policies, combined with a dramatic shift toward alternative energy sources for electrical generation, resulted in steep declines in domestic coal consumption starting in the 2010s. Whereas UP moved 2.16 million carloads of coal in 2011, traffic fell to just 1.23 million loads in 2017 and continued to decline. As late as 2020, UP was still moving almost 800,000 carloads of coal annually, and the Powder River Basin remained the largest domestic coal producer, representing more than 40% of coal mined in the U.S. In late 2021, rising natural gas prices and increasing energy demands saw increased output from Powder River mines, although with the projected closure of many coal-fired generating stations, the overall downward trend in coal traffic was expected to continue.

A livestock extra rolls eastbound behind 4-12-2 No. 9510 along the main line in central Nebraska near the east end of a center siding. In the 1940s, livestock moves were still an important part of UP's freight business, although over the next few decades this business withered.
A.C. Kalmbach

Historic perishable traffic

In Union Pacific's first century, perishable traffic (fresh fruits and vegetables) and livestock moves represented a significant portion of its carload freight. The specialized needs for accommodating perishables included expedited schedules, icing stations to keep cars cool, and facilities for watering animals en route. Complicating the challenge of car supply was the seasonal nature of most of this business.

Pacific Fruit Express was a joint venture between UP and SP that operated and maintained thousands of insulated refrigerator cars known as "reefers" that carried perishable traffic. PFE was formed in 1906 under the Harriman administration, and was one of only a few Harriman-era institutions that survived anti-trust actions. Reefers carried produce from packing houses across the far West to Midwestern and Eastern markets for distribution. Perishable trains known as "fruit blocks" consisted of bright orange PFE reefers that operated on fast schedules second only to passenger trains. Key areas included citrus from southern California groves, vegetables from California's San Joaquin and Salinas valleys, and various products from the lush agricultural regions of UP's territory across Idaho, Oregon, and Washington. In its early years PFE operated and maintained about 6,000 ice-bunker reefers. Its business grew rapidly, as at least some areas in its territory produced harvests year-round; the ability of reefers to deliver products across the country led to increased harvesting and production. By 1943, PFE's fleet had swelled to 40,800 refrigerator cars.

Before the advent of practical mechanical refrigeration, reefers were stocked with ice in bunkers (located at the ends of each car) to keep produce cool (salt was sometimes added when cooler temps were needed). This ice required replenishing on a daily basis in transit, so huge car-icing facilities were strategically located to ice trains as they worked their way east. PFE operated 18 such plants on UP and SP lines, the

An eastbound livestock extra is 3 miles west of Topeka, Kan., on the former Kansas Pacific on Dec. 3, 1949. Leading is 2-10-2 No. 5065, one of the UP's Lima 2-10-2s equipped with Young valve gear.
Don Smith

A westbound high-priority Z train snakes under Interstate 80 west of Reno, Nev., as it ascends Donner Pass on Nov. 10, 2003. The UP has since improved clearances on the route to allow double-stack trains. *Brian Solomon*

largest of which was at SP's Roseville yard where many fruit blocks heading east were assembled. PFE icing facilities on UP included Ogden, Utah, Laramie, Wyo., Cheyenne, Wyo., and one of the most significant, North Platte, Neb., which iced up to 1,000 cars daily.

Perishable traffic ebbed and flowed depending on harvest seasons, so there were several peak periods during the year. It was crucial at these times to have reefers in place and ready to move, as produce has very limited shelf life once harvested. During one seasonal peak, SP could deliver seven or more solid trains of reefers to UP at Ogden each day. Depending on the weight of trains, UP sometimes combined perishables trains at Ogden for the run eastward.

In the late-steam era, east of Ogden UP limited operation of fruit blocks to a maximum of 70 cars (about 3,200 tons). These were often hauled by the famous 4-8-8-4 Big Boys over the Wasatch Range. The UP's Challengers (4-6-6-4s) were often used on the more level territory east of Green River, and three-cylinder 4-12-2s east of North Platte. Yards to sort reefers were located at Laramie, North Platte, and notably Council Bluffs, Iowa. North Platte was the dividing point for traffic destined for Omaha/Council Bluffs or diverging at Gibbon Junction toward Kansas City. At Council Bluffs, perishable trains were broken up and cars interchanged with various eastern connecting railroads.

The growth of interstate highways and larger semitrailers hit PFE traffic hard by the 1960s. By the early 1980s, perishable traffic had almost entirely vanished. The advent and improvement of mechanical refrigerator cars in the 1950s and later led to removal of ice cars; the last icing dock was closed in 1973. In 1978 PFE was split between its owners, becoming Union Pacific Fruit Express and Southern Pacific Fruit Express. Some perishable traffic still moves across the Overland Route in mechanical reefers, but traffic is a shadow of the heyday of the steam and early diesel eras.

Livestock trains

Union Pacific had a long history of bringing livestock to market. Cattle, sheep, and pigs raised on the western plains required transport eastward to packing plants and stockyards in several cities, notably Kansas City, Omaha, and the famous Chicago Stockyards. As California's population grew through the 1930s, it became a major destination for livestock traffic as well. By World War II, Union Pacific was handling an enormous volume of livestock traffic westward over the LA&SL route to Los Angeles Union Stock Yards.

Livestock traffic originating across Wyoming, Idaho, Montana, and Utah was forwarded to Salt Lake City, where stock cars were assembled into trains known as Stock Specials for expediting to Los Angeles. In the steam era, these livestock trains required approximately 56 hours to run the 790 miles from Salt Lake City to

On Aug. 31, 1996, a westbound freight works through the Platte River Valley on the Kearney Subdivision near Kearney, Neb. *Brian Solomon*

The railroad made a massive investment in Centralized Traffic Control during and after World War II. Among the lines equipped was the heavily traveled, largely single-track route over the grades in eastern Oregon. At the LaGrande, Ore., dispatching office, a dispatcher is seated at CTC panels with the division superintendent standing at the left.
Union Pacific

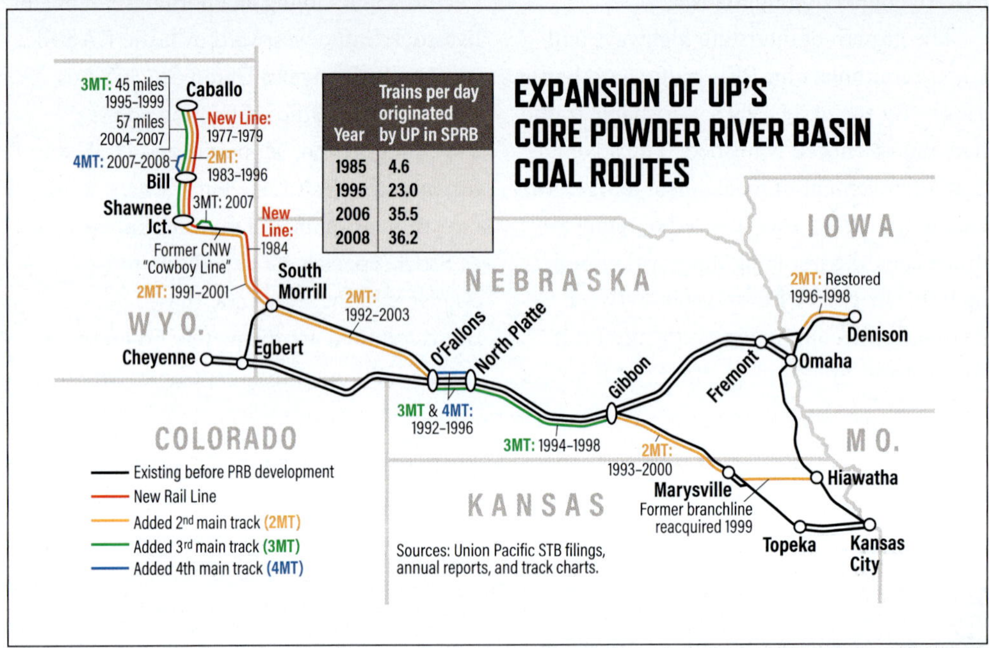

Year	Trains per day originated by UP in SPRB
1985	4.6
1995	23.0
2006	35.5
2008	36.2

Los Angeles. They were routinely hauled by 2-10-2s, but the trains needed helpers over the toughest grades. Federal laws mandated that for health of the animals they needed to be taken off trains at least once every 28 hours for food, water, and rest (at the option of the livestock owner this limit could be extended to 36 hours). Livestock was typically refreshed at Salt Lake City and again at Las Vegas.

Although UP's livestock trade was booming in the 1940s, it was starting to feel the sting of competition from trucks. Following World War II, UP improved its livestock operations by speeding the schedules of stock specials with the aid of wartime-installed Centralized Traffic Control and diesel operations on the LA&SL. During 1947 and 1948, the railroad rebuilt 800 stock cars with Timken roller bearings to minimize delays from hotboxes.

These changes allowed UP to dramatically cut the Salt Lake City-Los Angeles running time from 56 hours to just 27 hours, eliminating the need for most stock trains to pause at Las Vegas. This UP called this new train the *Daylight Livestock,* train No. 299. By 1949, livestock traffic accounted for about 3% of UP's freight volume; in 1951 the railroad carried 92,500 livestock loads, more than any other railroad.

The shift of packing houses from large cities to outlying areas (closer to feedlots and ranches) and the growth in truck traffic caused rail livestock traffic to plummit from the late 1950s through the 1960s. The UP kept some traffic, including westward hog movements in rebuilt triple-deck cars with built-in feed and watering troughs, but most traffic had disappeared by the 1980s. The UP was the last U.S. railroad to carry livestock, when a final push of traffic for Clougherty Packing Co. in Los Angeles ended in 1994.

Signaling and dispatching: Centralized Traffic Control

Push-button Centralized Traffic Control (CTC) was introduced in 1927. This method of train control blends the elements of interlocking and automatic block signaling by using relay logic circuits to give dispatchers complete control over lineside operations. By allowing trains to proceed on signal indication without the need for traditional authority—typically timetables and train orders—CTC permits a single dispatcher to authorize train movements over great distances (hundreds of miles in

A westbound empty unit coal train on the former C&NW approaches NI interlocking in West Chicago on Oct. 8, 1995. Among the peculiarities of C&NW operations were the preference for left-hand running and the use of horizontally oriented color-light signal heads. *Brian Solomon*

A westbound domestic intermodal train led by SD70ACe No. 8648 crosses the former Chicago & North Western through truss swing bridge over the west channel of the Mississippi River. The main structure the bridge was completed by Pennsylvania Steel Company in 1909. *T. S. Hoover*

many installations) with the push of buttons on a control panel. Although expensive to install, CTC increased the capacity and flexibility of single-track main lines without the need for station operators to deliver orders to trains at remote locations. The system allowed dispatchers to communicate operating authority directly to train crews without the need of middlemen.

During World War II, Union Pacific installed CTC on some of its busiest single-track routes to ease operating bottlenecks, reduce train times, and reduce employment. The Los Angeles & Salt Lake route was ripe for improvement. A vital line during the war, it was largely a single-track route, and it was saddled with a series of heavy grades while crossing hundreds of miles of some of the loneliest desert territory in the country. As wartime traffic to California increased dramatically, the route became congested. The UP worked with its primary signal supplier, Union Switch & Signal, to solve the problem. Initially, US&S installed 171 miles of CTC on UP's California Division, Third Subdivision, between Las Vegas and Yermo, Calif.—located three miles east of the junction of the LA&SL route and Santa

Fe's Needles District at Daggett, Calif. (To reach Los Angeles, UP operates via trackage rights on Santa Fe—today on BNSF—via Barstow, Calif., and over Cajon Pass to a junction at West Riverside, Calif.) The success of this CTC operation encouraged UP to install CTC in eastern Oregon on its OSL main line to the Pacific Northwest between Huntington and LaGrande, Ore., another heavily graded, largely single-track route that had reached capacity.

Sold on the benefits of push-button dispatching, UP invested in more CTC installations after the war. This included most of the LA&SL route between Salt Lake City and Las Vegas (about 350 miles). The original installation was controlled by UP dispatchers in Salt Lake City, which included the territory from west of Salt Lake City to Caliente, Nev., as well as the Cedar City Branch. The CTC west of Caliente to Yermo, Calif., was controlled from Las Vegas. Union Pacific continued to invest in CTC, using it to replace existing automatic block signaling installations as well as improving operations in previously "dark" (unsignaled) territory. Today most of the railroad's busiest routes are equipped with CTC-style signaling.

Union Pacific freights pass on California's Cajon Pass on Jan. 23, 2021. The train in the background works the former SP Palmdale Cutoff, while in the foreground an east-bound train led by UP No. 2557 is on the main line that's shared with BNSF from Daggett to West Riverside, Calif. *Bob Karambeles*

Tier 4-compliant General Electric ET44AH No. 2629 leads a Sunset Route east-bound along the Salton Sea on Feb. 27, 2019. The Sunset Route was one of the big prizes for UP in the 1996 merger with SP and today is among UP's busiest routes. *Bob Karambeles*

General Electric ES44AC No. 5496 leads an eastbound manifest up Donner Pass west of Cisco, Calif. The train is crossing the deck truss bridge in front of Red Mountain west of shed No. 10. Southern Pacific built the double-track bridge in 1904 during Harriman-era improvements to the Sierra crossing. *T.S. Hoover*

Cab signals

For many years, UP's traditional main lines westward from Omaha to Cheyenne and beyond were equipped with an automatic cab signal system that provided four-aspect, three-block protection. Coded signals sent through the rails give the locomotive engineer a continuous signal display in the cab. This reflected block occupancy ahead of the train and offered a greater degree of protection than traditional block signaling.

Chicago & North Western installed a two-aspect system with train control and without wayside intermediate signals on its Chicago-Omaha main line west of Chicago suburban territory. Between control points, train movements were governed strictly by cab signal. The two-aspect signals allow trains to proceed at "normal" or "restricted" speed depending on conditions ahead. This system was less flexible than UP's but still provided a higher degree of safety than conventional lineside block signaling. In 2022, with modern Positive Train Control safety systems in place on many lines, UP retired large sections of its older cab signaling systems, including the former C&NW systems that were deemed redundant.

Centralized dispatching

When Union Pacific opened its Harriman Dispatching Center in Omaha in June 1989, it was the first major American railroad to consolidate all train dispatching functions at a single centralized location. This $50 million project began in 1987 and required nearly two years to complete, but ultimately allowed the railroad to consolidate numerous positions and eliminate hundreds of jobs by closing eight regional dispatching centers—some of which were relatively new, having resulted from smaller-scale consolidations a few years earlier.

Positive Train Control

In 2008, Congress passed the Rail Safety Improvement Act, requiring major railroads across the U.S. to install advanced signaling and safety systems on lines that handle

On March 30, 2018, after cresting 4,196-foot Cima Hill summit on the LA&SL route, a westbound domestic intermodal train completes an "S" curve among the Joshua trees that dot Cima Dome near the west switch of Chase siding. Train operations over California's Cima Hill must adhere to special speed instructions based on train tonnage and locomotive braking effort. *T.S. Hoover*

passenger services and/or freights moving toxic inhalation materials. Qualifying safety systems, collectively known as Positive Train Control (PTC), were required. These systems are designed to prevent collisions between trains, overspeed derailments, train derailments caused by misaligned switches, and protect track crews in designated work areas. At the time of the act, there was no commercially available technology capable of meeting these requirements. The first deadline for implementation was mandated for the end of 2015; this was later extended to 2018.

The Union Pacific and other major freight carriers worked together with Wabtec to develop a PTC-compliant system called Interoperable Electronic Train Management System (I-ETMS), which was based in part on a prototype system developed by BNSF. Using specialized technology, I-ETMS can pinpoint individual train location, direction, and exact speed using on-board computers. Computers evaluate data supplied by radio and global-positioning input to provide advanced warning to locomotive engineers regarding the limits of operating authority, restrictive conditions, or specific safety hazards ahead of the train. PTC is designed to provide sufficient warning to allow engineers to take corrective action, and in situations where the engineer fails to act accordingly, PTC can bring a train to a controlled stop. The system was designed be applied as an overlay to existing signalling and dispatching systems.

By 2019, UP had invested nearly $3 billion in development and installation of operational I-ETMS along its lines and on its locomotives to cover approximately 17,000 route miles and 5,550 locomotives.

CHAPTER 5

EIGHT DECADES OF UP STEAM

Union Pacific operated some of the largest and most innovative steam locomotives in the U.S.

Union Pacific 2-8-0 No. 428 leads train No. 83 between Grand Island and Ord, Neb. This tri-weekly mixed train served Nebraska farm country, departing Grand Island, Neb., at 9 a.m. on Tuesdays, Thursdays, and Saturdays, taking just over three hours to reach Ord, 61 miles away. *Stan Kistler*

In its first 80 years, Union Pacific relied predominantly on steam locomotives to haul its trains. The railroad's steam power acquisitions can be loosely divided into three phases. The early steam era included 19th-century machines of various builder-driven designs. Steam in the early 20th century, during the Harriman era—when UP and SP shared management and resources—was characterized by engines built to the "common standard" plans. The last phase, modern steam, included several distinctive late-era designs to meet the demands of heavier and faster traffic; this pushed the steam locomotive to its ultimate development.

In each successive phase, the railroad demonstrated greater levels of involvement in the design process, culminating with unique UP locomotive types that were among the largest, most-powerful steam engines of their day. These magnificent engines have been the most interesting for locomotive photographers and historians because of their great power and size.

The railroad's late-era steam locomotives featured high-capacity boilers plus a host of modern equipment and appliances such as automatic stokers, feedwater heaters, advanced truck designs, lightweight rods, and advanced driving-wheel designs, plus roller bearings for axles and rods.

Classic American 4-4-0s

In many respects the UP's early steam power was typical for a mid-19th century American railroad. The backbone of its fleet was the common 4-4-0 American, assigned to all varieties of work from slow freights to passenger service. Union Pacific bought new locomotives from many builders, including Baldwin, Brooks, Cooke, Manchester, Norris, Rogers, and, of course, Schenectady. By the late 1800s, the railroad's Omaha Shops began to build new locomotives. Significantly, UP had always relied on coal for fuel, owing in part to the lack of suitable timber along its east-west route.

Union Pacific 4-4-0 No. 119 is among the railroad's most famous locomotives, representing the completion of the

In the mid-19th century, the 2-8-0 Consolidation emerged for heavy mainline freight service. No. 268 was part of an order of a dozen similar locomotives built in 1882 and early 1883 by Taunton Locomotive Manufacturing Co. of Massachusetts.
Brian Solomon collection

transcontinental railroad when it posed pilot-to-pilot at Promontory with Central Pacific's *Jupiter*.

The 4-4-0 offered agile and versatile operation over uneven track, with enough power to pull the small trains of the day, leading it to be the most-common locomotive type from the 1850s through the 1880s. Number 119 was built in 1868 by the Rogers Locomotive Works of Paterson, N.J., as part of an order for five similar engines. Rogers was a respected locomotive builder noted for producing high-quality machines characterized by detailed decorations. This coal-burning 4-4-0 was among the fleet of locomotives assigned to railroad construction and hauling supplies. It was an accidental player in the Golden Spike ceremony—UP's intended locomotive didn't reach Promontory in time, so No. 119 was drafted as a suitable alternative to represent the railroad.

More representative of Union Pacific 4-4-0s was the *Seminole,* a locomotive that author Alfred Bruce highlighted in his book *The Steam Locomotive in America* as a typical example of mid-century steam locomotives. Also a Rogers engine, it was constructed in 1867 with 16x22 cylinders and 54-inch driving wheels, and weighed 62,000 pounds (42,000 pounds on drivers). For its day, it was a powerful, compact locomotive utilizing the remarkable flexibility characterized by the 4-4-0's three-point suspension that helped make this a popular wheel arrangement. The 4-4-0 design was gradually superseded by larger, more-powerful locomotives in heavy service, although UP continued to assign 4-4-0s to branchline and specialized service into the 1900s.

Ten-Wheelers, Consolidations, and Mastodons

During the early years of the UP, the common 4-6-0 Ten-Wheeler was second only to the 4-4-0 in popularity, and 4-6-0s served on the railroad for almost 90 years, the greatest longevity of any wheel arrangement. Its third set of drivers and heavier weight gave the 4-6-0 more power than the 4-4-0. The UP bought its first 4-6-0s for freight service

Opposite page: American (4-4-0) No. 75 poses on the turntable at the Omaha roundhouse. This 4-4-0 was built by Rogers at Paterson, N.J., in 1868 and is typical of Union Pacific's early locomotives. Through the late 1800s the 4-4-0 was a jack of all trades and widely used by UP and its affiliated railroads.
American Geological Society

in 1867, assigning them to its mountainous main line across Wyoming where greater power was needed. Early 4-6-0s had 57-inch drivers—the smaller wheels were suited for applications where high tractive effort was required. The type soon supplanted the 4-4-0 for heavy service, and by the 1880s, the 4-6-0 was UP's standard freight locomotive. Although soon superseded in mainline freight service by more-powerful types, UP continued to purchase 4-6-0s into the early 20th century; a few examples remained on the roster for light work into the 1950s.

The UP was among the earliest roads to adopt the 2-8-0 Consolidation, buying its first examples just a couple of years after the type was introduced by Lehigh Valley in 1866. UP's first 2-8-0 was considered a big engine for its day; it weighed a third more than the typical 4-4-0 and was intended for service on tough grades out of Cheyenne, Wyo.

Union Pacific's largest 19th-century locomotives were 15 powerful 4-8-0 Mastodons built in 1899 by Cooke for UP's Oregon Short Line (OSL) and by Brooks for UP proper. The Brooks 4-8-

Os (class TW-57) were unusual among UP steam power because of their wide Belpaire fireboxes. Although common on many Brooks engines of the period (and standard on Pennsylvania Railroad and Great Northern), the Belpaire firebox with its prominent flat firebox crown sheet was rare on other lines. In their early years, UP's 4-8-0s worked either side of Cheyenne, moving freight over Archer and Sherman Hills; OSL's 4-8-0s worked on tough grades in Idaho and Oregon.

The 4-8-0 arrangement remained a curiosity on the UP system although the type found greater acceptance on Southern Pacific. Displaced by much larger power in the early 20th century, the 4-8-0s were retired during 1925 and 1926.

Compound 2-8-0s

In 1890, UP ordered Schenectady cross-compound 2-8-0 locomotives. These were UP's first compound steam locomotives, which had become a popular design variation using double expansion to improve

Consolidation No. 104 was built by Baldwin in 1895, and it outlasted similar 2-8-0s by a couple of decades. It was among antique steam locomotives assigned to Nebraska's Kearney Branch, where it worked until the early 1950s. It's shown at Grand Island, Neb., on July 5, 1951. *George C. Corey*

efficiency and conserve water. The cross-compound used an asymmetrical design whereby a small-diameter, high-pressure cylinder on one side of the locomotive exhausted into a larger diameter low-pressure cylinder on the other.

At the turn of the century, UP made a substantial investment in Baldwin 2-8-0s with the four-cylinder Vauclain compound arrangement, patented by Baldwin's Samuel Vauclain in 1889. It was distinguished by an arrangement of a pair of high- and low-pressure cylinders on each side of the locomotive, where each pair of cylinders were connected to a common cross-head to enable equal power to be delivered on each side of the engine. This overcame the disadvantage of unequal thrust which plagued two-cylinder cross-compound designs. Vauclain compounds gained popularity in the late 19th century, but the design's advantages ultimately didn't outweigh the added cost of maintaining more complex equipment. The locomotives were either converted to conventional simple operation or scrapped.

Harriman Common Standard locomotives

Under the visionary administration of Edward H. Harriman, the UP and SP systems—jointly known as the Associated Lines—changed the way the railroads designed and purchased locomotives. Harriman believed in the value of central authority and aimed to plan, design, and purchase large numbers of locomotives to standard specifications with common parts among different types of engines. The goals were reduced construction

The three-cylinder 4-10-2 was the vision of UP's chief mechanical officer A.H. Fetters, who in the mid-1920s worked with Alco in their design. Alco built 10 for the railroad, numbered in the 8000/8800 series; they were rebuilt as conventional two-cylinder engines during World War II and renumbered 5090-5098. No. 5093 is at Salt Lake City on Aug. 20, 1952. *John E. Pickett collection*

costs and reduced maintenance expenses (by minimizing the cost of replacement parts and reducing the need to stock or manufacture component parts custom-designed for individual engines).

In summer 1902 the Associated Lines Joint Committee was formed to establish standards (in addition to UP and SP, this grew to include Chicago & Alton and Kansas City Southern). The SP's mechanical department was assigned the task of drafting Common Standard designs and starting in 1903 they made plans for 10 standard locomotive types, setting detailed standards for every component of those locomotives.

Working from this, locomotive purchases began about 1904. From 1907 onward the Union Pacific Equipment Association had the responsibility for procuring most new motive power for Harriman lines. Placing huge orders with various builders not only lowered engineering costs, but allowed railroads to get volume discounts. Ultimately, hundreds of locomotives were built for UP and SP under this joint arrangement. Although Harriman died in 1909, locomotive standardization continued for a few more years and had lasting effects even after the forced anti-trust breakup of UP and SP. Many locomotives ordered during this period operated until the end of the steam era.

Standard 2-8-0s and 2-8-2s

The Union Pacific system (including its various primary and subsidiary affiliated railroads) invested in hundreds of standardized 2-8-0 Consolidations. Beginning in 1904, UP system 2-8-0s were built to Harriman Common Standard plans (classes C-1 and C-2). These 20th century 2-8-0s were far more substantial locomotives than UP's early 19th century wood-burners. They were larger and more powerful, and spartan in overall appearance compared to earlier examples of the type. Although UP stopped investing in new 2-8-0s by 1910, when it switched to buying 2-8-2s for mainline freight, some of its standard 2-8-0s served secondary roles until the 1950s, when they were finally displaced by diesels.

Among the most common steam locomotive types on the UP system before dieselization was the 2-8-2 Mikado. This wheel arrangement was adopted as a new standard heavy locomotive and widely built from 1910 through World War I. Ultimately nearly 500 2-8-2s served the UP, classes MK-1 to MK-10. Where many railroads bought 2-8-2s exclusively for freight, UP initially used 2-8-2 for both freight and passenger service.

The earliest Mikados came with 57-inch drivers; later locomotives used 63-inch drivers. Most of the Mikados were built to UP specifications, although during World

The prototype 4-12-2 Union Pacific locomotive, No. 9000, is working freight at Lexington, Neb., in the early 1950s. The 4-12-2 was unique to UP. Not only was it the largest three-cylinder engine built—it was also the most-numerous class of three-cylinder steam locomotives on any U.S. railroad. *John E. Pickett*

War I, UP acquired 20 Mikados built to United States Railroad Administration design (class MK-Special).

Mallet articulateds

A Mallet (pronounced "malley") is an articulated compound, where high pressure cylinders on the rear engine exhaust into larger low-pressure cylinders on the forward engine. Union Pacific ordered six 2-8-8-2 Mallets from Baldwin in 1909 (class MC-1). Early Mallets such as these were powerful machines intended for slow-speed, heavy freight service in graded territory; the UP's largely worked the Oregon grades. They were scrapped in the mid-1920s.

In 1918, Union Pacific ordered 15 2-8-8-0s from Alco-Schenectady (class MC-2). These were more successful than the 2-8-8-2s. Repeat orders brought the total to 70 (nearly a third of all 2-8-8-0s built) by the mid-1920s (classes MC-3 to MC-6). Many were assigned to heavy freight service in Wyoming, and to grades on the OSL and OWR&N where the greater tractive effort was needed. Beginning in the 1930s, the railroad converted them to simple (non-compound) operation. Some survived until the mid-1950s.

2-10-2s

A significant phase in UP's development of big freight power was its extensive purchases of the 2-10-2 type, beginning with a sample order of 10 locomotives from Baldwin in 1917. The type was known nationally as the Santa Fe in acknowledgment of that railroad's pioneering use of the arrangement; however, UP avoided naming the class for a chief competitor, and so referred to its fleet simply by the wheel arrangement. They were classified as TTT (two-ten-two). UP purchased more 2-10-2s between 1920

Alco 4-12-2 No. 9047 leads an extra freight with stock cars and reefers that had been holding on a center siding on UP's busy main line in Nebraska. At the time, the Omaha-Ogden main line was largely directional double-track protected by automatic block signals in the form of lower-quadrant semaphores. *A.C. Kalmbach*

and 1924 from all three major builders, ultimately buying 185 of the type. Engines from consecutive orders were numbered in sequences from 5000 to 5524. Despite overall similarity of design—all with 63-inch drivers—there were many variations among orders when it came to the application of appliances, the type of valve gear, and of tenders. A few were briefly equipped with trailing truck booster engines.

All of the TTTs were bought for heavy mainline freight service, designed for faster speeds and greater tonnage than older locomotives. Initially, they were assigned to the difficult territory between Cheyenne, Wyo., and Ogden, Utah, but the TTTs ultimately worked across the UP system, from desert grades on the Los Angeles & Salt Lake to long freights over the Encina, Telocasset, and Kamela grades in eastern Oregon to level territory across eastern Wyoming, Kansas, and Nebraska. In later years, when premium freight assignments had been assumed by more modern engines, the TTTs found work system-wide handling a variety of secondary freights and working as helpers.

Significantly, the 2-10-2s were UP's first locomotives equipped with automatic stokers, a necessity on such large engines. Engines 5040 to 5089 were unusual: They were equipped with Young valve gear instead the more common Walschaerts gear. They were the largest single application of Young gear, which derived its valve control motion solely from cross-head connections. The design was intended for large locomotives; its goal was better control when starting heavy trains and maintaining sustained fast running without a dramatic increase in fuel or water consumption. Results were mixed; the Young gear was also used on UP's 4-8-2s. Interestingly, the Young gear experiment was tried on engines built by Alco, Baldwin, and Lima.

Early 20th century passenger power

The 4-4-2 Atlantic type was developed in the 1890s for fast passenger service to better handle the longer and faster trains of the period. It was named for the Atlantic Coast Line (the first user), and was popular on Eastern railroads. Union Pacific was a relatively late buyer of the type. Its first were ordered in 1903, and were an early product of Harriman's Common Standard designs. The UP system acquired 35 4-4-2 Atlantics (classes A1-A4), many with 81-inch drivers for fast service in level or lightly graded territory where the relatively light engines could dash along. Others were built with 70-inch drivers for service on the LA&SL grades. Where some railroads invested first in 4-4-2s and then supplanted them with more-powerful 4-6-2 Pacifics, UP was unusual in that it simultaneously acquired 4-4-2s and 4-6-2s for different applications depending on traffic demands.

UP's first 4-4-2s were the class A-1s ordered in 1903, and delivered in batches beginning in 1904. Its class A-3s were Baldwin Vauclain compounds built in 1906, and the final Atlantics were 15 class A-4s, built in 1911. The Atlantics performed well in their early years, but they were poorly suited for the heavy all-steel cars and longer and heavier consists of the World War I period. Unsuited for other service, the tall-drivered 4-4-2s were largely retired in the 1920s.

The 4-6-2 Pacific became a common passenger locomotive on the UP system in the first decades of the 20th century. Built from 1904 to 1920, UP rostered 13 classes (P-1 to P-13). All the major builders supplied 4-6-2s built to Common Standard plans. All were built with 77-inch driving wheels, but other details differed. Most received Vanderbilt tenders, easily identified by their cylindrical tanks. In their early years the Pacifics were assigned to long-distance passenger trains west of

Extra 9020 West eases out of the center siding at Kimball, Neb., behind a 4-12-2 on July 5, 1951, having just been overtaken by the westbound *Pacific Limited*, train No. 23. *George C. Corey*

Cheyenne, but they were bumped from these assignments when 4-8-2 Mountains were delivered in the early 1920s. For a time they worked territory formerly held by the Atlantics. In later years some were modernized with lightweight alloy-steel rods, lightweight driving wheels, and roller bearings on the main axles. Although gradually displaced by more powerful engines, some Pacifics worked secondary trains until the mid-1950s.

Pacific No. 2906 was renumbered 49 and rebuilt as a streamliner in 1937, along with 4-8-2 No. 7002. Both were shrouded with styled sheet metal and painted in brown and gold livery to work the home-built streamliner *Forty-Niner* (Omaha-Cheyenne). These were UP's only conventional reciprocating streamlined steam locomotives. After the *Forty-Niner* was discontinued in 1941, the shrouds were removed and the locomotives returned to conventional appearance.

Mountains

The 4-8-2 Mountain type first appeared on Chesapeake & Ohio to haul heavy passenger trains on its Appalachian grades. Some railroads, notably New York Central, adapted the 4-8-2 for fast freight. Union Pacific bought 4-8-2s for heavy passenger service, specifically to move its heaviest trains more quickly in territory with stiff grades. Alco built 70 4-8-2s between 1922 and 1924, which UP used to supplant its Pacifics and passenger-service Mikados. Initially 15 4-8-2s were assigned to the Los Angeles & Salt Lake. First of the type was Class MT-1, No. 7000, which was typical of UP's 4-8-2s. Like all of UP's Mountains, it had 73-inch drivers. As-built they had large cylindrical Vanderbilt-style tenders riding on six-wheel trucks, with capacity for 12,000 gallons of water and 20 tons of coal. The UP had these built with the unusual Young valve gear about the same time that it ordered its freight-service 2-10-2s with Young gear. In

No. 3558 was among UP's compound 2-8-8-0s rebuilt as simple engines in the 1930s. The rebuilding extended their service lives, and some operated into the early 1950s, often working as helpers on heavy freights. *John E. Pickett*

Union Pacific's 4-8-4s, class FEF, were designed under Otto Jabelmann and built by Alco. They were considered among the finest of the type ever built, and designed for 90-mph operation. No. 813 was one of 20 FEF-1s delivered in 1937. It had 77-inch driving wheels; later 4-8-4s had 80-inch drivers. *John E. Pickett collection*

the mid-1930s, the railroad rebuilt many of its 4-8-2s, replacing the Young gear with the more common Walschaerts and adding an advanced front end, one-piece cast frames, and integral cylinders. The last of the Mountains were retired in 1956.

Three-cylinder simples: 4-10-2 and 4-12-2

In the 1920s, Alco promoted advanced three-cylinder simple locomotives (high pressure steam directly from the boiler to all cylinders) as way of hauling more tonnage at faster speeds without materially increasing engine size or weight. Initially, Alco sold three-cylinder locomotives to several Eastern railroads, but UP and SP were both interested in larger designs and encouraged development in the form of a new 4-10-2 arrangement. UP's first experimental 4-10-2, No. 8000, was tested in heavy freight service and delivered results impressive enough to warrant mention in the trade press. The May 1926 issue of *Railway and Locomotive Engineering* reported that UP's 4-10-2 hauled "twenty per cent more tons in regular service, with an expenditure of sixteen per cent less fuel per thousand gross ton-miles." Both UP and SP ordered fleets of 4-10-2s, which became known as Overlands. The UP's nine were initially assigned to freight service on its graded LA&SL.

However, before these were even delivered, UP worked with Alco to expand the design and ordered another experimental locomotive (No. 9000) with the previously untried 4-12-2 wheel arrangement. Alco delivered this long-boiler locomotive to UP in 1926 (ahead of production 4-10-2s). They were named the Union Pacific type—and the UP would prove to be the only railroad to own them. The UP was impressed with the 4-12-2 arrangement and ultimately ordered 87 more (Alco's largest single order for three-cylinder engines). UP's early 4-12-2s were built by Alco's Brooks Works, the last major order built there. The remainder were built by Alco's Schenectady plant.

The 4-12-2s were huge locomotives. They featured a 30-foot 8-inch wheelbase—the longest on a rigid-frame American steam locomotive. To effectively negotiate tight curves, Alco installed lateral motion devices on the forward and rear driving axles and blind (flangeless) drivers on the third and fourth axles. Nevertheless, the inflexibility of the wheelbase placed serious limitations on where the locomotives were allowed to operate, excluding them from some secondary lines and tight yard trackage.

The Union Pacific type was remarkably successful and long lived; the engines outlasted all other American three-cylinder locomotives in mainline service. The 4-12-2s excelled at pulling heavy freights at speed in level, straight territory, and UP routinely assigned them to road freights on its Nebraska main line into the mid-1950s. Although most were scrapped, the prototype was preserved and is displayed at Pomona, Calif.

Challengers

Union Pacific's 4-6-6-4 Challenger type, first built by Alco in 1936, was an important milestone in the evolutionary advancement of articulateds, and is credited as the first successful heavy articulated locomotive for sustained fast service. During the 1920s, the concept of a simple articulated was developed to produce a much more powerful locomotive. The key was designing a locomotive with ample boiler capacity to supply both the rear and forward engines with high-pressure steam directly from the boiler, enabling higher speed and more

Union Pacific No. 844 is among the railroad's best-known locomotives. It was UP's final steam passenger locomotive and its only steam locomotive never retired from service. It was photographed in fresh paint at Cheyenne on Nov. 20, 1960. It remains on the active roster in 2022. *John E. Pickett*

Big Boy No. 4003 was suffering from a plugged flue so Challenger No. 3940 was sent to assist. Both are seen eastbound on Sherman Hill in July 1951. At the back of the train was Challenger No. 3937 working as a helper. *George C. Corey*

power than a Mallet compound.

Alco was a leading proponent of simple articulated designs and in the late 1920s pushed the limits of this type. In the 1930s, UP approached Alco to develop a flexible high-output locomotive that could equal or exceed its 4-12-2s, and that could operate at top speeds without the curve limitations of the 4-12-2's long wheelbase.

UP Assistant General Superintendent of Motive Power and Machinery Otto Jabelmann worked with Alco's designers on the new 4-6-6-4 design. Features included modern lightweight alloy steel for reciprocating parts (including side and main rods) which significantly reduced potentially destructive reciprocating forces (known as dynamic augment). Roller bearings were applied to locomotive and tender axles.

The four-wheel leading truck provided good front-end stability and the four-wheel trailing truck was essential to a large firebox. Other improvements included precise weight distribution between forward and rear engines to allow for better balance at high speed. The 4-6-6-4s featured 69-inch drivers and 22" x 32" cylinders. They proved to be an adaptable locomotive capable of speeds up to 80 mph, with flexibility allowing it to operate on most main lines.

UP named the 4-6-6-4 the Challenger type shortly after adopting the *Challenger* name for its innovative Chicago-Los Angeles train. Ultimately UP took delivery of 105 4-6-6-4s—the largest Challenger fleet built. UP's later Challengers benefited from an improved suspension, with a lateral bearing surface supporting the forward engine with

Challenger No. 3937 works as a helper on an eastbound freight ascending Sherman Hill at Hermosa, Wyo., in July 1951. Big Boy No. 4003 and Challenger No. 3940 are leading.
George C. Corey

minimal vertical movement, making it among the most stable of American articulated locomotives. The UP's Challengers were capable of hauling more than 7,000 tons on level ground, but were most desirable in graded territory and so were routinely assigned west of North Platte. They were common on the LA&SL route, where they were assigned to passenger as well as freight trains.

A few Challengers were equipped with "elephant ear" style smoke deflectors to minimize problems with smoke and exhaust gases entering the cab. Tenders on early Challengers rode on pairs of six-wheel Buckeye trucks; later tenders featured 14-wheel "centipede" trucks. Two UP Challengers were preserved; in 1981, UP restored No. 3985 for service on excursions.

Big Boy

In the steam era, it was common practice to develop a locomotive type for a specific application. In the late 1930s, UP needed a better way of hauling "fruit blocks"—solid trains of refrigerator cars carrying perishable traffic—moving east from the SP interchange at Ogden. These time-sensitive, heavy trains were UP's fastest scheduled freights, expediting agricultural products from California and Oregon to Eastern and Midwestern markets. A chief obstacle was the eastbound grade over the Wasatch Range. As perishable traffic grew, UP had resorted to

Challenger No. 3985 is one of two surviving UP examples of the type. This massive Alco 4-6-6-4 was restored to operation in 1981 and is pictured leading a National Railway Historical Society trip near Livermore, Calif., on UP's former Western Pacific line over Altamont Pass on July 19, 1992. *Brian Solomon*

double-heading heavy trains east of Ogden, a costly, inefficient solution.

In 1939, Electro-Motive introduced its four-unit, 5,400-hp model FT freight diesel. Although UP was an early proponent of diesel-electrics in passenger service, it continued to view steam as the backbone of freight operations. So rather than embrace the FT, the railroad worked with Alco to design an even more-powerful steam locomotive capable of hauling eastbound perishable trains solo from Ogden.

The solution was expanding upon the successful 4-6-6-4 design by increasing the boiler size and adding two pairs of drivers to create a 4-8-8-4. The result was a massive machine—the largest locomotive built until that time—weighing 772,000 pounds. With its tender it measured 132 feet 9⅞ inches long. Although big, it was also flexible: Articulation allowed the engine to negotiate 20-degree curves.

The type was impressive, but what really caught the public imagination was its name. David P. Morgan in the August 1952 *Trains & Travel* related the story of an Alco shop employee who wrote "Big Boy" in chalk on the smokebox door of a 4-8-8-4 under construction. Years after the end of the steam era, it was revealed that Chesapeake & Ohio's massive 2-6-6-6 Alleghenies (constructed after UP's Big Boys) were actually slightly heavier.

Big Boys were modern locomotives,

Stand back and feel the thunder as double-headed Challengers, Nos. 3953 and 3937, lead an extra west-bound freight at Ozone, Wyo., in July 1951. *George C. Corey*

The first of the Big Boys, No. 4000, is at Cheyenne, Wyo., on Oct. 9, 1953. Built by Alco in August 1941, it was off the roster by 1961. *John E. Pickett collection*

equipped with roller bearings on drivers and some reciprocating parts, and with cylinders integrally cast with the locomotive frame. Like the Challenger, the Big Boy could deliver ample quantities of steam to maintain sustained power at high speed. It featured enormous steam pipes to channel steam from the boiler to the cylinders. The Big Boy was intended for fast freight and, despite its size, could easily reach 70 mph—although in regular service a 55 mph top speed was more typical. It was at its most powerful when running at about 30 mph. The first 4-8-8-4 was delivered to Union Pacific at Council Bluffs, Iowa, on Sept. 4, 1941, and it entered service a few days later leading a 100-plus-car train.

Like the Challenger, the Big Boy awed observers. Author Alfred Bruce estimated Big Boy's maximum output at close to 7,500 hp, a figure significantly greater than the 5,400 hp of Electro-Motive's new four-unit FT (although the FT had greater starting tractive effort).

Because of their exceptional length, UP's Big Boys were restricted from many turntables and other servicing tracks, limiting where they could be assigned. Typically Big Boys worked mainline freights between Ogden and Cheyenne, and occasionally from Cheyenne to Denver.

In 1943, author S. Kip Farrington Jr. traveled on Big Boy No. 4015 running eastward from Ogden. His notes offer a glimpse of the locomotive's performance: "This trip departed Ogden at 1:15 p.m. with 69 cars representing 3,190 trailing tons. At Echo, Utah, the train paused at 2:51 p.m. to take on coal and water, continuing on its eastward journey at 3:14 p.m. The engine was serviced at Evanston, Wyo., taking 20 minutes, and was again replenished with coal and water at Carter, [Wyo.], where it paused for just 11 minutes. It arrived at Green River, Wyo., at 9:40 pm, where the train dropped some cars and swapped out [No.] 4015 for a 4-6-6-4 Challenger-type number 3961, before continuing east."

Union Pacific bought 25 Big Boys from Alco across two orders, in 1941 and 1944. The Big Boys survived later than most steam, moving trains over Sherman Hill as late as 1959. Their enormous size has made them among the most famous American locomotives despite their relatively few numbers and obscure service. Today eight of

On July 4, 1951, Union Pacific Big Boy No. 4020 leads an eastbound freight over Wyoming's Sherman Hill. *George C. Corey*

the locomotives are preserved, some rather far from where they operated. Union Pacific famously restored No. 4014, returning it to operation in 2019.

Class FEF 4-8-4s

Union Pacific adopted the 4-8-4 Northern wheel arrangement later than other big Western railroads. Northern Pacific and Santa Fe pioneered the type in the 1920s, while UP didn't order 4-8-4s until the late 1930s. The railroad finally adopted the 4-8-4 for mainline passenger service when its trains grew and required more power than its 1920s-era 4-8-2s.

UP's first 20 4-8-4s, Nos. 800-819, were built by Alco in 1937. UP classed them as FEF ("four-eight-four"). By any measure, the 800s were thoroughly modern steam power, and were among the finest 4-8-4s ever built. They had one-piece cast integral frames, 77-inch Boxpok lightweight drivers, Timken roller bearings on all axles (a first for UP), and valves with needle bearings.

UP worked with Alco to refine its 4-8-4 design, placing additional orders that were delivered in 1939 and 1944. UP's final 4-8-4s were among the most-impressive passenger steam locomotives built in the United States. They had 80-inch Boxpok drivers counterbalanced for 110 mph, with 100-square-foot firebox grates and 300-pounds per square inch boiler pressure. They were designed to work at 90 mph with 1,000-ton passenger trains. One of the things that distinguished UP's 4-8-4s was their exemplary service records. Many averaged 15,000 miles per month, and while they were ordered primarily for passenger service, they also worked freights.

Most famous of UP's 4-8-4s is No. 844, the last in its class, built by Alco in 1944. After the end of regular steam operations, UP retained 844 in serviceable condition. It has operated on many high-profile excursions and special trains, and remains on the active roster in 2022.

CHAPTER 6

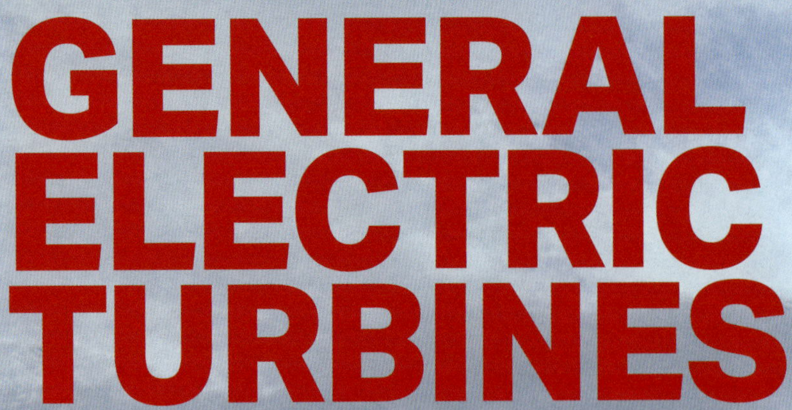

GENERAL ELECTRIC TURBINES

Union Pacific's unique turbines provided more power than diesels of their era

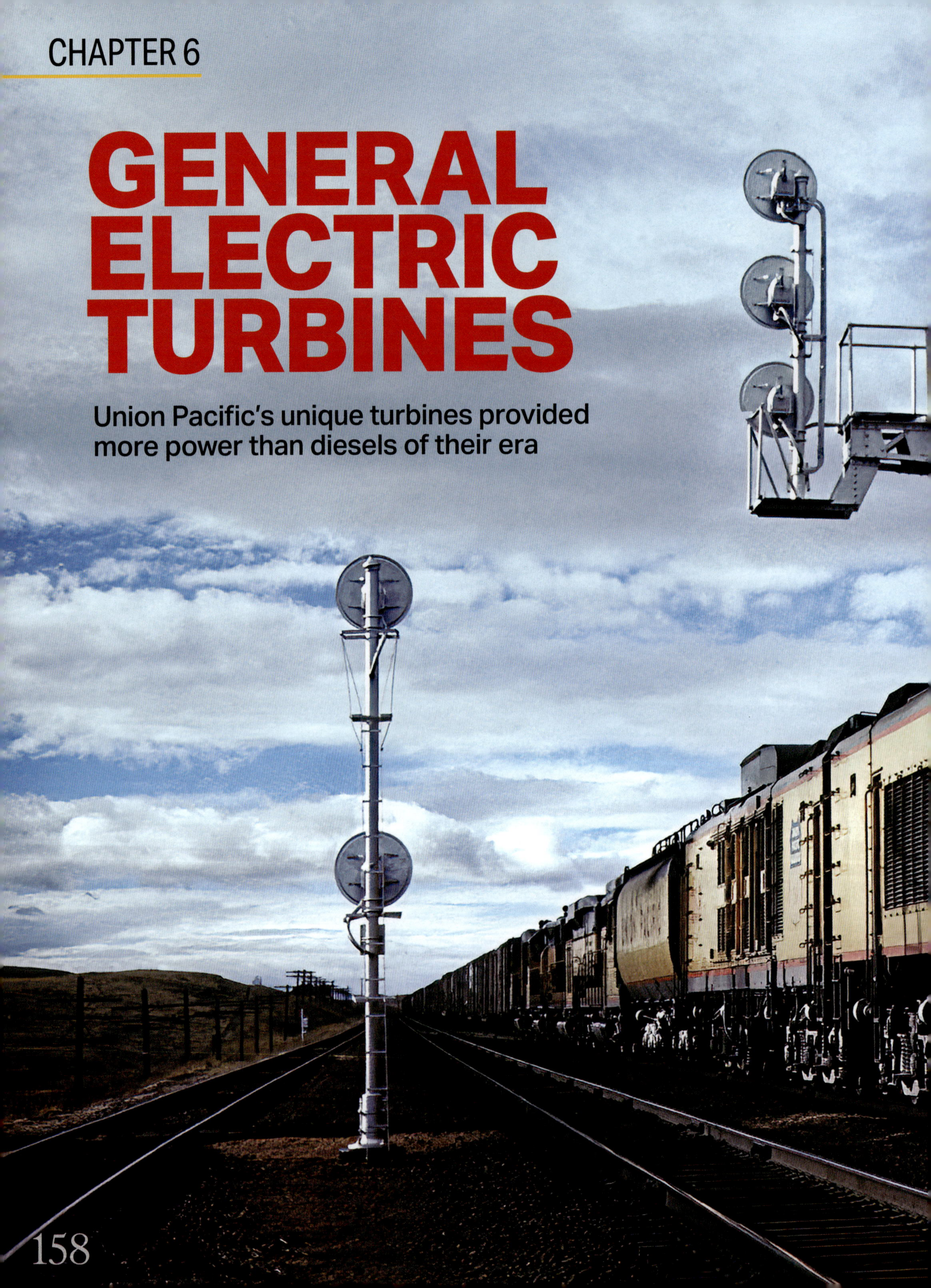

An eastbound led by 8,500-hp turbine No. 26 and four GP30 and GP30B diesels—17,500 hp total—gets the signal to proceed toward Cheyenne, Wyo., in December 1966. At the peak of their service, UP claimed the turbine fleet was hauling almost 15% of its annual ton-miles. By 1970, the turbines were finished, doomed by age, the rising price of Bunker C oil, and advances in diesel-electric technology.
Mel Patrick

Union Pacific has long been an innovator with motive power. Examples include early diesel streamliners; novel and extremely powerful reciprocating steam locomotive designs; and large twin-engine diesel-electric power. Union Pacific's exploration into new types of locomotives notably embraced General Electric's development of high-horsepower, turbine-electric locomotives, and beginning in 1936, Union Pacific worked with GE in development of an oil-fired steam turbine-electric.

General Electric was a leader in advanced stationary and marine steam turbine technology, and in the 1930s combined this with existing electric locomotive technology to design and build of a pair of streamlined steam turbine-electric locomotive prototypes. Each engine of the pair rode on a 2-C-C-2 wheel arrangement (two unpowered guiding axles, two sets of three powered axles, and two unpowered trailing wheels). Each unit was rated to deliver 81,000 pounds of starting tractive effort and 2,500 hp. This was substantially more powerful than existing diesel-electric designs of the period, and GE hoped that it would have twice the thermal efficiency of conventional reciprocating steam power. The prototype was three years in the making, and in spring 1939 GE's powerful steam-electric was presented to UP for tests. The trade press at the time promoted it as the latest in futuristic locomotive designs.

The streamlined steam-electrics were intended to operate "elephant style" rather than back-to-back. External styling was similar to UP's early diesel streamliners, but featured a prominent 9-foot projecting nose. The body was a lightweight truss frame constructed from welded alloy steel covered

General Electric's oil-fired steam turbine-electric locomotives of the late 1930s were among the most impressive looking locomotives to work UP rails. Unfortunately, UP found that the reliability of the powerful locomotives didn't equal their appearance, so their operations were short-lived. *Union Pacific*

UNION
PACIFIC
THE
OVERLAND
ROUTE
UNION

Turbines Nos. 1 and 2 lead a passenger special past lower-quadrant semaphores on the Lane Cutoff a dozen miles west of Council Bluffs, Iowa in 1939. These big oil-fired steam turbine-electrics were designed to carry passenger trains at 100 mph or move freight on heavy mountain grades. *Brian Solomon collection*

with riveted sheet metal. The sides were aluminum, while the nose sections were made from steel for greater strength and collision protection. Each unit was 90-feet, 10-inches long and 15-feet, ¾-inch tall.

The locomotives employed Babcock & Wilcox automatic high-pressure (1,500 pounds per square inch) water-tube boilers. These required highly purified water, operated in a closed circuit, to minimize boiler scale and reduce the volume of water consumed by the locomotive. Water lost during the heating cycle was replenished from tanks in each locomotive nose; fuel oil tanks were located at the rear of each locomotive.

They had an unusual form of dynamic braking: By directing boiler water through a circuit heated by dynamic-brake resistor grids, the engine conserved a portion of the energy generated during braking. This led to better overall thermal efficiency and lowered fuel cost. GE introduced another innovation: a head-end electric generator designed to supply electricity to passenger cars for heat, light and air conditioning—decades before head-end power was standard for American passenger equipment.

The locomotives' service time on UP was brief, but widely publicized. In May 1939 the railroad used them to publicize the 70th anniversary of the Golden Spike, operating special trains that toured the system and also went offline to Eastern cities. The steam-electrics were impressive on paper and awed the public with their streamlined styling, but they suffered from a variety of mechanical failings and UP quickly soured on their lack of reliability. The railroad scuttled plans to assign the turbines to a high-profile transcontinental passenger runs and instead returned them to GE after the publicity tours. Ultimately the railroad opted to focus on more-reliable motive power. The combination of American involvement in World War II, the railroad's investment in Big Boy steam locomotives, and the debut of Electro-Motive's FT freight diesels effectively ended UP's interest in the steam turbines.

Gas turbines

After World War II, GE furthered its development of turbine locomotives, and in 1948 constructed an experimental double-cab, oil-fired, gas-turbine-electric (GTEL) prototype for testing on UP. Despite the nationwide move toward dieselization, UP was interested in gas-turbine power because of the potential for a single unit to deliver substantially greater power than commercial diesel-electrics while burning lower-grade

Built by GE at Erie, Pa., this one-of-a-kind twin-cab 4,500-hp experimental gas-turbine-electric locomotive was painted for UP and given No. 50. It spent months testing on UP, and ultimately led to the railroad's order for 10 similar single-cab units. *General Electric*

No. 55 is one of 10 single-cab, 4,500-hp gas-turbine-electrics built by GE in 1952. These GTELs were on the UP roster until 1962, when they were traded in to GE for U50 diesels. *Union Pacific*

(cheaper) fuel oil. The power potential of a gas-turbine appeared to suit UP's needs of pulling long, heavy, fast freights hundreds of miles between terminals. Advantages of gas-turbines included greater power output for the weight of the locomotive; simpler mechanical components to allow for greater reliability and lower maintenance cost; and rapid acceleration.

Union Pacific tested GE's prototype, which was painted in the railroad's colors and numbered 50. This massive machine weighed nearly half a million pounds, was 83-feet, 7½-inches long, and more than 15-feet, 4-inches tall. It had a B-B+B-B wheel arrangement (all axles powered), similar to some GE heavy electrics, and was rated at 4,500 hp—three times that of a single contemporary EMD F3 diesel.

The locomotive was powered by a gas-turbine engine adapted from GE's aircraft design. The engine turned four GE-576 generators. The electrical transmission system was similar to that used by contemporary Alco-GE diesel-electrics, with which it shared common components, including GE-752 traction motors on each axle. A six-cylinder Cooper-Bessemer diesel provided auxiliary power for starting the turbine and for moving the locomotive at slow speeds.

The UP was more patient with No. 50 than it had been with the steam-electric turbines. It worked with the prototype for about a year and half, covering more than 100,000 miles in heavy service across the system. During this time the GE engineering team addressed a variety of minor technical faults and issues that UP found objectionable. Finally satisfied with the prototype in 1950, UP moved forward with a plan to operate a fleet of similar units in Overland Route freight service between Council Bluffs, Iowa, and Ogden, Utah.

The railroad ordered 10 units (Nos. 51-60), delivered in January 1952. These were similar to the prototype but saved space and cost with a single cab. Difficulties with air compressors were overcome by using a motor-driven design. Success with these led to a second order of 15 (Nos. 61-75), delivered in 1954. Built to a more-advanced design, they featured external running boards ("catwalks") along the sides, and became known as Veranda Turbines.

Still happy with the turbines, UP in the mid-1950s ordered an additional 30 units (Nos. 1-30) to replace the 25 Big Boy 4-8-8-4s, which were nearing retirement. These turbines, delivered in 1958, were significantly more powerful at 8,500 hp. They were characterized by a 132-foot, 6-inch long, two-section carbody, with each section riding on C-C trucks. The leading section featured the control cab, auxiliary diesel engine and electrical generator, fuel tanks, auxiliary equipment, and dynamic braking grids. The rear section carried the turbine, main generators, and related primary electrical equipment. The 12 axles (six below each section) were each powered by a GE-752 traction motor. For greater service range, the railroad added a 23,000-gallon fuel tender—recycled from retired steam locomotives—to each turbine.

Gas-electric turbine No. 52 is about to cross the Green River with a freight from Ogden as it approaches the Green River, Wyo. yard. Among the advantages of GE's gas-electric turbine locomotives was the ability to generate high horsepower by burning low cost Bunker C fuel oil.
Union Pacific

No. 1 was the first of UP's 8,500-hp gas-electric turbine locomotives. A total of 30 of these extraordinarily powerful "super turbines" were built by GE in 1958, Nos. 1-29. They were advertised as "the most powerful locomotives ever built," and some were later uprated to 10,000 hp.
Union Pacific

In the twilight of GTEL operations on the UP, an 8,500-hp turbine leads a westbound extra freight past the station at Ogallala, Neb., on April 19, 1969. *Mel Patrick*

Demise of the turbines

The gas-turbine era was brief. Turbine-electrics were extraordinarily efficient compared to diesel-electrics, but they only delivered optimum efficiency at maximum load, with efficiency falling off dramatically as turbine speeds decreased. The railroad's plan was to operate the turbines exclusively on long-haul, heavy freight runs; however, the real-world environment of mainline operations didn't always allow them to work at maximum efficiency.

A key of the turbines' efficiency, since they burned *a lot* of fuel (about double that of an equivalent diesel), was their use of Bunker C fuel oil. Bunker C is a low-grade, heavy oil that cost only a fraction of diesel fuel, but its viscous nature required heating it to 200 degrees to get it to flow properly. By the late 1950s, greater efficiencies in oil refining allowed getting more valuable products from Bunker C; the material also became a feedstock for refining into plastics—an industry that was booming by the late 1950s. This caused Bunker C prices to rise significantly, eliminating any cost savings of using it as locomotive fuel.

Number 26, an 8,500-hp turbine, works eastward through Ogallala, Neb., in March 1968. It would be retired less than two years later, but escaped scrapping. It survives on display in Ogden, Utah. *Mel Patrick*

In what would be an ear-splitting scene, in September 1966, gas-electric turbine No. 2 and a GP30 lead a westbound stock extra in the climb over Wyoming's Sherman Hill west of Cheyenne on main track no. 3. *Mel Patrick*

The final group of 8,500-hp turbines were paired with 24,000-gallon fuel tenders converted from old steam locomotive tenders. The tenders gave the locomotives a truly massive appearance.
Trains collection

EXPERIMENTAL COAL TURBINE

Eying rising Bunker C prices, and with high-horsepower twin-engine diesels still in their early days, the Union Pacific in late 1962 began experimenting with a coal-fired gas turbine. The UP built an experimental locomotive (No. 80; later 8080) using a retired Alco PA as the control unit, retaining its diesel engine, a body from a Great Northern W-1 electric locomotive to house the turbine, and a coal tender from a retired Challenger steam locomotive.

The UP encountered many of the same problems and challenges of the experimental coal turbines of Chesapeake & Ohio and Norfolk & Western in the early 1950s, namely turbine blade corrosion from ash and the difficulties of grinding and handling coal. As railroads kept discovering, coal turbines are great for large stationary installations, but unworkable in tight spaces on moving platforms. The locomotive made several runs but was ultimately unsuccessful; in early 1968 it was disassembled with various components scrapped or traded in.

The last chapter in UP's turbine motive power was this experimental home-built coal-fired turbine locomotive constructed from parts from various retired locomotives. It's at Council Bluffs, Iowa, in September 1966; it was scrapped in 1968. *Mel Patrick*

Another difficulty became the deafening noise of turbine operation, an unceasing roar likened to a steam locomotive boiler being blown down (or standing next to an aircraft jet engine), which contributed to the turbines' uncomplimentary moniker of "Big Blows." Unacceptably high noise levels ultimately limited where the locomotives could be assigned. The turbines were also complex, requiring a high level of care and maintenance, and mechanical issues began increasing as they grew older.

By the early 1960s, advances in diesel-electric technology made it possible for diesels to more closely match the performance and efficiencies offered by GTELs without all the shortcomings associated with turbine operation. Also by 1960, GE was competing directly in the North American diesel-electric market and was offering some of the most-powerful diesels available. In 1963, UP traded the 4,500-hp turbines back to GE for U50 diesels. Most of the 8,500-hp GTELs were traded in between 1969 and 1971 for new U50Cs, recycling key components such as trucks. The bodies of a couple of turbines were preserved: No. 18/18B is at the Illinois Railway Museum in Union, Ill., and No. 26/26B is among UP rolling stock displayed at Union Station in Ogden, Utah.

Although relatively short-lived, the turbines delivered several years of good service to UP. They were fascinating machines, and they certainly represent the railroad's desire to experiment with alternative technology and operate large, powerful, fast locomotives.

CHAPTER 7

DIESEL LOCOMOTIVES

Union Pacific has operated a variety of unique diesel-electric designs

The Union Pacific rostered more SD40-2s than any other railroad, and they could be found leading priority mainline trains for more than three decades. On Aug. 13, 1978, two eastbound freights are at Bosler Hold, Wyo. No. 8072 was one of the railroad's "Fast 40s"—SD40-2s renumbered to the 8000 class to reflect 59:18 gearing for speeds up to 83 mph. On the right is Extra 3454 East, led by a conventional 3000-series (numbered to match horsepower) SD40-2 with standard 65-mph gearing. *Brian Jennison*

As with steam locomotives, Union Pacific has been a pioneering and progressive railroad with diesels. The UP was the first to put an internal-combustion streamlined passenger train in service—the Pullman/Electro-Motive M10000—and followed it with several other diesel streamliners. The UP dabbled in models from all builders as it dieselized through the 1950s, and was known for its input in developing high-horsepower, twin-engine diesels in the 1960s. Its diesel fleet today includes the most modern Tier-4 compliant-locomotives on the rails.

Passenger diesels

Soon after its first diesel streamliners entered regular service in the early 1930s (see Chapter 3), Union Pacific realized the limitations imposed by fixed-consist, articulated, single-ended trains. The railroad and GM's Electro-Motive Corp. also recognized the value of stand-alone diesels that weren't tied to specific trains or consists. Meanwhile, GM's engineers in the mid-1930s were working to improve basic locomotive technology (engine, generator, traction motor, and body). This led to the design and production of high-speed, streamlined diesel locomotives—the E series—incorporating the best characteristics of the early streamlined power cars and boxcab diesel designs while introducing a host of significant innovations.

In 1936, UP ordered six E2 diesels in two A-B-B sets (cabless B units). Delivered in 1937, the E2 model was distinctively styled and unique to UP, although functionally identical to EA and E1 models built concurrently for Baltimore & Ohio and Santa Fe. One set (SF-1, -2, -3) was to lead the Chicago-Oakland, Calif., *City of San Francisco* (operated with Chicago & North Western and Southern Pacific); the other set (LA-1, -2, -3) for the *City of Los Angeles,* run with C&NW. As-built, SF-1 carried a chrome shield on the front exhibiting the emblems of Union Pacific, Chicago & North Western, and Southern Pacific. When joint operation involving the *COSF* was dissolved in 1948, one of the *City of San Francisco* E2As was conveyed to SP, becoming its 6011A, and later repainted in SP's Daylight livery.

New Fairbanks-Morse Erie-Built diesels were among the displays at the June 1947 Car Builders Convention in Atlantic City, N.J. These shiny new 2,000-hp units were shipped to UP in August 1947 and initially had 63:24 gearing for passenger service. *Trains magazine collection*

The E units featured several improvements over earlier integral power cars, including a redesigned air intake system—UP's early streamliners had huge nose intake grilles; at speed, this unfortunately tended to force debris into the engine compartment. This problem was alleviated by repositioning intake vents to the locomotive sides.

The E units featured elevated cabs behind a slanted nose, and they rode on newly designed, innovative high-speed, three-axle A1A trucks (center axle unpowered) designed by Martin Blomberg. The Es were two-engine locomotives; each 12-cylinder, 900-hp Winton 201A diesel drove its own generator, supplying power to one truck, for 1,800 hp per unit. (Electro-Motive's "E" designation came from the *E*ighteen hundred horsepower output of the original models.) The UP was the only railroad to order E2s, and they were characterized by a longer and more rounded (bulbous) nose, plus distinctive rows of porthole windows on the sides.

As UP expanded its fleet of streamlined trains, it purchased more passenger locomotives, relying mainly on Electro-Motive E units. Prior to World War II, this included E3s (2) and E6s (8), both of which were 2,000-hp diesels featuring a slanted nose and powered by pairs of upgraded EMD model 567 diesel engines. After the war, UP placed orders for successive E unit models, including E7s (14), E8s (46), and E9s (69), respectively rated at 2,000, 2,250, and 2,400 hp. The railroad's final E9s were delivered in 1964, making them the last new carbody-style passenger diesels built by EMD.

Union Pacific preferred six-axle passenger locomotives for its long-distance trains, in contrast with several other Western lines that relied on four-axle F units for passenger service (including future UP properties Western Pacific and Rio Grande). The UP did, however, have a group of steam-generator-equipped F3s (11 A units and 16 Bs) delivered in 1947-1948, plus two FP7s (matched with F7Bs) that were delivered in 1952.

Union Pacific received two orders of Alco-GE passenger engines (later known as PAs and PBs) in 1947 and 1949: eight PAs and six PBs. The six-axle PAs had a distinctive nose and body styling, and

Opposite top: The Union Pacific bought a small fleet of Electro-Motive E6 passenger diesels (eight A units, 4 Bs) in 1939 and 1940. In their early years the E6s filled in where needed to haul UP's streamlined passenger trains. The original odd hyphenated numbering soon gave way to conventional numbers; No. 7-M-1 eventually became 992. *Electro-Motive Corp.*

Union Pacific's 11 Alco RSC2s were originally numbered 1180 to 1190. Designed for lightweight track, they weighed 235,000 pounds and rode on A1A-A1A trucks (center axles unpowered), for 156,600 pounds on driving wheels. The locomotives were rated at 1,500 hp. *Alco*

differed from EMD's E units by having single engines (16-cylinder Alco 244 diesels rated at 2,000 hp). The Alcos were typically assigned to secondary passenger trains between Cheyenne, Wyo., and Los Angeles, including the *Utahn, Los Angeles Limited,* and *Pacific Limited.* In 1955, Union Pacific regeared the PA/PBs for freight service in Nebraska and Kansas, and in 1959, UP converted PA No. 608 into the cab of multiple-section, experimental, coal-fired gas turbine number 80 (later 8080).

Six-axle Fairbanks-Morse Erie-Builts—known as such because they were assembled at General Electric's Erie, Pa., plant—first arrived in December 1945, and UP would receive eight A units and five Bs through 1947. These carbody locomotives were FM's equivalent to the EMD E7 and Alco PA. Each unit was powered by a 10-cylinder opposed-piston diesel rated at 2,000 hp. They were geared for 75 mph and intended for heavy freight service, but UP was soon dissatisfied with their freight performance. In 1946, UP regeared them for 102 mph and assigned them to Los Angeles & Salt Lake passenger trains. In 1955, they were again regeared and reassigned to freight service; all were retired by the early 1960s.

After World War II, Union Pacific ordered a pair of Baldwin's DR12-8-3000 "Centipedes." These massive carbody diesels measured 91-feet 6-inches long and had an unusual 2-D+D-2 wheel arrangement. Although the two massive locomotives were completed by Baldwin (and to be numbered as UP 998 and 999), UP canceled the order before delivery.

The UP's last new passenger diesels were 10 dual-service EMD SDP35s built in 1965. These road switchers were basically SD35s with steam generators at the rear of the long hood. When Amtrak was formed in 1971, the SDP35s were less than six years old, so UP kept them and used them in freight

No. 1341 is one of three 1,600-hp Fairbanks-Morse H16-44s bought in 1950 (Nos. 1340-1342); the UP had earlier acquired five FM H15-44 road-switchers in 1948 (Nos. 1325-1329). In their early days these were among locomotives that had the letters "DS" for "diesel switcher" ahead of the road number. *Union Pacific*

service. They remained on the roster until 1985, but had been stored by 1980.

Freight diesels

Despite being a pioneer with early passenger diesels, UP was notably reluctant in purchasing diesels for freight service until after World War II. By that time UP's competitors, notably Santa Fe and Burlington, had successfully demonstrated the advantages of Electro-Motive FTs in freight service. Union Pacific began acquiring road freight diesels during the mid-1940s, but continued to rely on its big, modern steam power and GE gas-turbines for heavy freight work; UP was initially less reliant on diesels for mainline freight than other Western lines. Ultimately, diesel-electric technology prevailed, and by the early 1960s UP was operating the world's largest and most-powerful single-unit diesel-electrics.

Union Pacific didn't invest in EMD's popular freight-service F units until 1947, almost eight years after the first FT made its debut. The railroad placed its first order for 1,500-hp F3s in 1947, and—pleased with their performance—acquired a total of 142 freight versions of the model through 1949.

Despite being the most-common model of the UP's early dieselization period, UP's large fleet of EMD F3s was largely ignored by enthusiast photographers who instead eagerly sought to capture the railroad's modern steam in action. *Trains magazine collection*

In 1963, UP's lone Baldwin DRS6-4-15, No. 1250, is on the Omaha Shops scrap line with an Alco FA. Originally a Baldwin demonstrator, it was equipped with a steam generator for passenger service. It joined UP's roster in 1948.
Jim Seacrest

UP then followed by purchasing 56 of EMD's follow-up model, the F7, through 1953. The railroad's F3s and F7s were equipped with dynamic brakes for use in graded territory.

In 1958, the Union Pacific embarked on one of the country's first major diesel rebuilding projects, sending 84 F3s to EMD for upgrading to F9 specifications; UP and EMD both considered these to be new locomotives, even though some components were reused. Internally, the locomotives were completely rebuilt with new engines and electrical gear, emerging as 1,750-hp locomotives. Externally, they largely retained their original F3 appearance except for some details (such as 48-inch-diameter dynamic brake fans and an extra louver on each side ahead of the forward porthole).

During 1947-1948, UP also acquired a fleet of 90 Alco-GE FA1/FB1 carbody freight units. The four-axle, 1,500-hp diesels were powered by Alco's 12-cylinder 244 engine with GE-752 traction motors, noted for reliability. Like the F units, the FAs/FBs were dynamic-brake equipped. Among other places, these worked the main line between Council Bluffs, Iowa, and North Platte, Neb., and later were mainly assigned to the LA&SL west of Salt Lake City.

Early road switchers

Following World War II, UP sampled several road-switcher models from Alco, Baldwin, and Fairbanks-Morse. Electro-Motive was a relative latecomer to road-switcher production, not introducing its popular GP7 until 1949, but by the mid-1950s EMD products would represent the largest share of the UP diesel fleet.

Early road switcher acquisitions included 11 Fairbanks-Morse 2,000-hp H20-44s built in 1947 and powered by F-M's two-cycle, 10-cylinder, opposed-piston engine. In their early careers they were assigned to helper service on Cajon Pass. A year later, UP acquired an additional five F-M road switchers, H15-44s rated at 1,500 hp. The F-Ms lasted into the mid-1960s.

The railroad turned to Alco for two groups of 1,500-hp road switchers in 1947 and 1948: six RS2s (four-axle trucks), and 11 relatively rare RSC2s (A1A, four motor, six-axle trucks). The RSC2 offered lighter axle loading and was designed for light-rail branch lines. The UP's Spokane International affiliate bought 13 of Alco's 1,000-hp RS1s during 1948-1949.

Among the rarest locomotives on the railroad's early diesel roster were seven Baldwin road switchers: six 1,600-hp AS616s (six-motor) and one 1,500-hp model DRS6-4-1500 (A1A trucks) equipped with a steam generator.

Most significant were UP's first EMD road-switchers: 30 1,500-hp, four-axle GP7s and 10 1,500-hp, six-axle SD7s bought in

This 1950s view shows a new Alco FA diesel inside the railroad's new Council Bluffs, Iowa, diesel shops. *Union Pacific*

Union Pacific GP9 No. 303 works the yard at Yakima, Wash., in June 1978. The overhead wires were for electric locomotives operated by UP affiliate Yakima Valley Transportation Company. Electric freight operation ended in 1985. *Thomas L. Carver*

Union Pacific understood the flexibility and versatility of the building-block principle afforded by road switchers. The UP ordered from EMD hundreds of GP9s, including 125 cabless GP9Bs. *EMD*

You just know this sounded great! A sextet of SD24s and SD24Bs powered by turbocharged 16-567D3 diesels approaches Hermosa Tunnel on Sherman Hill leading a loaded coal train from Hanna, Wyo. in August 1973. *Mel Patrick*

1953. The railroad's experience with these dependable and versatile locomotives, which became known as Geeps—along with earlier F units—led it to purchase a sizable fleet of Electro-Motive road switchers over the following decades.

Between 1954 and 1957, UP invested in more than 300 GP9s. This 1,750-hp model supplanted the GP7 and ultimately proved to be one of the best locomotives of the postwar era, crucial to the building-block philosophy of locomotive allocation and assignment. Like the GP7, a GP9 could work by itself or in multiple-unit sets with other engines, and was at home working branch lines, yards, or the main lines. The railroad's unsatiated desire for power resulted in lengthy lash-ups of GP9s, and to help lower per-unit cost, UP ordered a significant fleet of the cabless model GP9B.

By the late 1950s, UP wanted more-powerful single units than the GP9s, so its Omaha Shops rebuilt some GP9s by replacing the Roots blower with a turbocharger, which boosted output to 2,000 hp. This alteration was so so successful that it spurred EMD's move to turbocharging, and the manufacturer in 1959 introduced its 2,400-hp, six-axle SD24 and 2,000-hp GP20. The UP bought 30 GP20s and 75 SD24s, including 45 cabless B units. In their early days these were assigned to the LA&SL where they worked the mountainous route between Salt Lake City and Los Angeles. As the GP20 gave way to the 2,250-hp GP30, UP bought 106 of them (40 cabless) in 1963, then bought 24 of the next model, the 2,500-hp GP35, in 1963 and 1964.

Union Pacific had been a regular Alco customer through the steam era, and bought

On a misty January day in 1977, DD35A No. 77 leads a pair of Southern Pacific SD45s at UP Junction in Tacoma, Wash. UP's 15 DD35As were delivered in 1965, a year after its 30 cabless DD35s (a model sometimes listed as "DD35B"). *Thomas L. Carver*

A prototype for the SD40 was the so-called model SD40X of 1965. These featured the new 16-645E3 diesel engine, but built on the shorter frame that had been used for the SD35 and with large angled radiator intake housings that gave them an appearance similar to the SD45. In 1966, UP bought eight of these (Nos. 3040-3047). *Union Pacific*

a fair number of early Alco diesel switchers and cab units. However, the railroad shied away from the builder in the 1950s. It returned to Alco briefly in the 1960s for token purchases of high-horsepower diesels. In 1961 UP bought four Alco RS27 demonstrators. These were four-axle road switchers, 2,400 hp, that were a precursor to Alco's Century line. UP's final Alco order was in 1966: 10 six-axle, 3,000-hp C630s, which the UP sold in 1973.

General Electric dissolved its diesel-electric partnership with Alco in 1953, although it continued to supply Alco with electrical components. In the meantime GE, which had produced several successful switching locomotives, developed its own high-horsepower road switcher to compete with Alco and EMD. The result in 1960 was GE's model U25B, a four-axle, 2,500-hp diesel powered by GE's FDL16 engine. In 1961, GE's U25B high-hood demonstrators toured the country. Union Pacific was among the first customers, buying 16 of them (including four former demonstrators) in 1961-1962.

An oddball locomotive on UP started life in 1954 as a GE experimental locomotive. Used as a test bed, GE built a single four-unit, carbody-style locomotive arranged in A-B-B-A configuration. The carbodies featured fluted sides. It was tested on the Erie extensively; GE later rebuilt the locomotives, designated them as UM20B, and sold them to UP in 1959. They remained on the roster until 1963.

Double diesels

The increase in diesel locomotive horsepower by the 1960s, combined with UP's desire for significantly more-powerful locomotives, led UP to encourage each of the remaining builders (Alco, EMD, and GE) to develop "double-diesel" models. These massive locomotives were effectively two locomotives on one long platform, with two engines and two generators under control of a single throttle. It was, theoretically, a relatively straightforward way of supplying much greater power in a single unit without the need to introduce dramatically larger prime movers and generators.

The cabless GP30B was another model unique to Union Pacific, which bought two batches from Electro-Motive in 1963 totaling 40 units (700B-739B). None of these oddballs diesels survive; all were off the roster by the end of 1983 and sold for scrap. *EMD*

General Electric's first offering was its model U50, a 5,000-hp locomotive powered by a pair of 16-cylinder FDL diesels, making it effectively two U25Bs on a single frame. It rode on four AAR Type B trucks in a B-B+B-B arrangement (trucks that had been recycled from traded-in first-generation gas turbines), with span bolsters above each truck pair. The U50 (sometimes incorrectly called "U50D") measured 83-feet 6-inches long and employed a distinctive cab with a stub nose that was shorter than those on other diesels of the period. The UP bought 23 U50s between 1963 and 1965; they were retired in the mid- to late-1970s. The only other railroad interested in the U50 was Southern Pacific, which bought just three examples.

In the late 1960s, GE revised the design, placing it on a long frame over six-wheel (C-C) trucks trucks recycled from the last generation of gas turbines, creating the U50C. The UP was the only customer, buying 40 from 1969 to 1971. The U50C was designed to improve reliability and efficiency. It was shorter and lighter than the U50, using 12-cylinder FDL engines but still putting out 5,000 hp. The radiators were back-to-back at the center of the hood; on the U50, one was directly behind the cab and the other at the end of the hood. Unfortunately, the U50C used aluminum wiring, which caused serious electrical failures (and many fires) within just a few years of service. Rewiring them proved prohibitively expensive; most were scrapped in 1977 and 1978, not even reaching 10 years of service.

Electro-Motive's first double diesel, the DD35, was effectively a pair of GP35s on one long (88-foot 2-inch) frame, powered by a pair of 16-cylinder 567D3A turbocharged engines for a total output of 5,000 hp. EMD approached truck design differently than GE, employing a new design: the four-axle Flexicoil (all axles powered), giving the locomotives a D-D wheel arrangement. The UP's first order, in 1964, was for 27 cabless DD35s (SP also bought examples), followed by an order for 15 cab-equipped DD35s. An unusual feature of UP's DD35As was that most were built with GE 752 traction

Oddball GE experimental cab units were at Lincoln, Neb., in March 1960, leading Extra 620 West—a train detouring over Burlington because of flooding. GE used them for testing; after being rebuilt and redesignated UM20B, the units were sold to UP in 1959. They were retired in 1963. *Jim C. Seacrest*

On April 9, 1969, GE U50 No. 48 passes block signals as it works the main line east of North Platte, Neb. The massive U50 rode on two pairs of trucks recycled from first-generation gas turbine locomotives. *Mel Patrick*

motors recycled from traded-in Alco FA/FB diesels. Most of these big diesels were scrapped between 1979 and 1980.

Union Pacific was happy with the initial performance of the big EMDs, and in 1965 EMD proposed an upgraded model using the new, larger 645 diesel engine just released for the GP40 and SD40. The DD40 was to be powered by twin 16-cylinder 645s and rated at 6,000 hp. Although EMD commissioned stylized drawings of DD40, it was never produced. However, in 1969 UP revisited the idea and EMD built an experimental model designated DDA40X. It was the largest and most powerful diesel-locomotive in the world. Along with its size—98 feet 5 inches—the DDA40X had several innovations. By increasing engine rpms, horsepower output was boosted from 3,000 to 3,300 hp (6,600 hp for the locomotive) using the turbocharged 16-645 engine. It used modular solid-state electronics in place of hard-wired relay circuits (features that became standard three years later on EMD's Dash-2 line) The DDA40X also used a full-width "cowl" style nose with a large two-piece windshield.

Union Pacific bought 47 DDA40X locomotives. With them, the railroad continued its long-standing tradition of assigning significant road numbers to

The first dozen of UP's 16 GE U25Bs were built with high short hoods, including four demonstrators that became UP Nos. 633-636. The remainder had low noses (UP and Frisco were the only railroads to buy high-hood U25Bs). In 1961, GE posed four new UP U25Bs near its plant at Erie, Pa. *General Electric*

noteworthy locomotives by giving them the 6900 series to mark the centenary of the Golden Spike in 1969. They became known as Centennials, although many observers knew them as Jacks. After a decade of mainline work, the DDA40Xs were among locomotives stored during the 1979-1980 recession. Most returned to service in 1984 to help move a surge of freight traffic, but they were then retired in early 1985.

Alco's double-engine offering was merely a footnote. In 1964, Alco delivered three eight-axle C855s (one B unit), each 86-feet long and powered by two 16-cylinder 251-series engines for 5,500 hp. The model was UP exclusive. They were neither reliable nor popular among crews, and they served only a few years before being scrapped in 1970.

Standard high-horsepower diesels

Having ordered fleets of unusual, specialized, and in some cases highly engineered but relatively high-maintenance locomotives during the 1950s and 1960s, Union Pacific changed its motive power philosophy by the early 1970s. The railroad began focusing the majority of its new locomotive acquisitions on standard EMD and GE 3,000-hp, six-axle models. By that time, the railroad had decided that the overall versatility, reliability, and relatively high power output of standard models (compared to 1950s and early 1960s diesels)—especially EMD's designs—outweighed any advantages of pushing the limits of high-horsepower specialized locomotives.

The new EMD 645 engine, introduced in 1966, was powerful and popular, and it established a new plateau for reliability. The UP bought GP40s with the 645 engine, but began relying on six-axle diesels—led by the SD40—for mainline freights. By 1971, the railroad had 123 SD40s, plus eight experimental SD40X diesels built in

1965. The UP also tried EMD's highest-horsepower single-engine model, the 3,600-hp SD45, buying 50 of them in 1968. This model used a 20-cylinder version of the 645 engine. The UP found that their increased fuel consumption and added maintenance weren't worth the extra horsepower, so they returned to buying SD40s instead; most of the SD45s were sold or retired by 1980.

Electro-Motive revamped its line in 1972 with its Dash 2 series, which had the same base models but with modular electrical components and many other internal improvements. Starting that year, UP began amassing the largest fleet of SD40-2s—more than 680 in several orders through 1980. The UP also inherited hundreds more SD40-2s as result of its mergers in the 1980s and 1990s. For more than two decades this model represented the backbone of UP's heavy freight fleet, and it was hard to find a train that didn't have at least one in the locomotive consist.

Variations included units numbered in the 8000 series in the mid-1970s that were regeared for 83 mph service (later renumbered and returned to the general pool) and locomotives that carried radio-control equipment in an extended-length ("snoot") nose section for service as radio remote helpers and helper control units.

Although not as common as the SD40s and SD40-2s, UP also bought large numbers of GE six-motor diesels beginning in 1966 with 10 U28Cs (2,800 hp). More popular were 150 U30Cs built between 1972 and 1976 and 140 of GE's upgraded C30-7 locomotives from 1977 to 1980 (all 3,000

The first EMD double-diesels were cabless DD35s; UP and Southern Pacific were the only buyers. Unlike Alco and GE, EMD came up with a new truck for its big diesels—a four-axle Flexicoil design. Here a GP35 leads a pair of DD35Bs shortly after they were delivered. *Union Pacific*

In September 1966, GP35 No. 762 leads an A-B combination of twin-engine Alco C-855s on an extra eastbound freight near Cheyenne, Wyo. Alco's model C-855 was unique to Union Pacific. *Mel Patrick*

hp). Although UP's U30Cs were retired in the 1980s, many C30-7s survived until the late 1990s, and a few into the early 2000s. The GEs could be found on mainline freights but were most common on unit coal trains.

GP38-2, GP40X

In the 1970s, the UP bought a fleet of GP38-2s and a handful of the experimental GP40X models from EMD. During 1974-1975, it received 60 GP38-2s, a 2,000-hp road switcher that was the 1970s equivalent of the GP9. These were logically placed in the 2000 number block. More unusual were six GP40X units built in late 1977 and early 1978. These were powered by the 3,500-hp F version of the turbocharged 16-645 engine. In place of the standard Blomberg B truck, these rode on experimental HT-B trucks that were designed to achieve higher adhesion. The GP40X was a foot longer than a typical GP40-2, and had large, angled radiator intakes similar in appearance to those on the SD45.

Microprocessor diesels

With its new Dash-8 line in the late 1980s, General Electric advanced diesel-electric technology by using onboard microprocessor controls to optimize fuel efficiency and increase locomotive reliability. The eventual success of that and other features of the new models eventually enabled GE to overtake EMD as North America's leading locomotive supplier. Locomotives in the Dash 8 line employed refined versions of GE's FDL engine and 752 traction motors, but with a new alternator/rectifier system and a refined modular approach to wiring and control systems that eased troubleshooting and maintenance. The UP hadn't played a major role in road testing GE's Dash 8 prototype locomotives, but in late 1985, through its ownership of Missouri Pacific, UP bought some advanced GE C36-7s (Nos. 9000-9059), rated at 3,750 hp, that incorporated elements of Dash 8 design.

The railroad was suitably impressed and placed an order for the 4,000-hp Dash 8-40C; UP's No. 9100 was the first production unit delivered in 1987. (The railroad classified them as C40-8.) The UP was happy with their performance and eventually placed five orders for the model, totaling 256 units, then acquired another 77 through the C&NW merger in 1995. They worked in a road pool, although in their early days they could often be found in matched sets along the railroad's original transcon line, carrying trains that three decades earlier had been led by GE turbines. The Dash 8s were distinctive with

Only Union Pacific could produce such an unusual consist of second-generation Electro-Motive diesels: an SD45, GP30B, and SD40-2 work Seattle-bound freight No. 691, using trackage rights on Burlington Northern's line along the shore of Puget Sound at Steilacoom, Wash. in June 1979. *Thomas L. Carver*

their sharply angled cabs compared to earlier GEs, and were easily spotted in consists.

SD60, SD60M

Electro-Motive had stumbled in diesel development in the early 1980s with its 50-line, which was an attempt to get higher horsepower output from its existing 645-series engine. The resulting GP50 and SD50 models suffered from a variety of mechanical and reliability issues, and UP avoided the models (but acquired some of each through merger).

EMD's new line of 60-series locomotives in 1984 was the manufacturer's attempt to overcome the technical failings of its 50-series. The SD60 was powered by Electro-Motive's new, larger 710 diesel engine. Like GE's Dash 8 line, EMD's 60-series benefited from a modern computer-controlled electrical system. The series also introduced desktop-style controls, replacing the traditional control stands of earlier diesels.

Between 1986 and 1988, UP bought 85 of the six-motor, 3,800-hp SD60; it would get another 55 in 1995 with the C&NW merger. UP was an early advocate of the North American Safety Cab, a modern wide-nose style that had its origins in the full nose-width cab applied to its DDA40X diesels, but reinforced with heavier-gauge metal and posts for better crash protection. The UP ordered EMD's safety-cab-equipped SD60M on the heals of its SD60 order. Built starting in late 1988, the first 184 of these locomotives (Nos. 6085-6268) featured an interim cab design characterized by a row of three forward-facing cab windows. Later SD60Ms—97 built starting in late 1991—featured a cab with just two windows.

GE safety cab Dash 8s

GE's adaptation of the North American Safety Cab was offered as an option for new locomotives beginning in 1989. UP initially ordered 50 Dash 8-40CWs that shared most of the same specifications as earlier Dash

The railroad bought 10 of Alco's big 3,000-hp Century 630s; they arrived in two batches of five in 1966. The first arrivals are pictured at the Council Bluffs (Iowa) Shop in late 1966. All 10 were sold to Duluth, Missabe & Iron Range in 1973. *Mel Patrick*

8-40Cs but with the wide-nose cab, Nos. 9356-9405. All subsequent GE road diesels built for UP would have the safety cab design.

The railroad followed up on its success with these GEs by placing repeat orders for the builder's slightly more powerful Dash 8-41CW model (UP class C41-8W, Nos. 9406-9664), ultimately acquiring 154. These can be spotted by a more ergonomically friendly angled step design, with five steps instead of four.

Dash 9 and AC4400CW

In the mid-1990s, GE upgraded its standard locomotives, bumping horsepower to 4,400 and officially making the North American Safety Cab as standard. The company offered both the standard DC-traction-motor Dash 9-44CW and its first AC-traction-motor locomotive, the AC4400. The UP invested in both models (as did both C&NW and SP shortly before they became part of UP).

In 1994, UP bought 40 Dash 9-44CWs (class C44-9W, Nos. 9700-9739), while sampling three similar looking, but technologically advanced AC4400CWs (C44AC, originally Nos. 9997-9999). The Dash 9 represented a refinement to Dash 8 technology, while the AC4400CW was a technological leap forward and GE's first AC-traction diesel, built in response to EMD's SD70MAC (for which UP competitor Burlington Northern had been the driving design force). Electro-Motive teamed up with Siemens AG to develop polyphase AC traction, while GE advanced its own AC propulsion technology based on its earlier work for transit applications.

The AC traction motor offered many advantages, including better adhesion and durability—it's almost impossible to overload an AC motor. However, the technology between controlling DC and AC motors is significantly different, and until the advent of microprocessor controls, AC traction wasn't

A pair of DDA40X Centennials lead an eastbound freight at Hermosa, Wyo. The DDA40X had a variety of distinctive features, including the pronounced gap in the hood between the engines, a cowl-style wide nose, and extreme length. These measured 98 feet 5 inches from end to end, the longest of any U.S. diesel. *Mel Patrick*

General Electric's final double-diesels were the 40 U50Cs built from 1969 to 1971. They had six-axle trucks and centrally placed radiators in the middle of the hood. *Louis A. Marre collection*

feasable on a locomotive. Simplified, AC traction motor control was made possible by high-voltage frequency-control equipment called inverters. Where the EMD system used one inverter for each truck (each inverter supplying three motors), GE's system featured six inverters per locomotive, regulating power to each axle individually. This provided higher tractive effort, was more reliable, and afforded superior wheel slip control which allowed greater adhesion and better dynamic braking. The AC motors also require less maintenance, which helps to lower operating costs.

Centennial No. 6908 shows off its distinctive D-style four-axle/four-motor Flexicoil truck as it races along in May 1980.
Mel Patrick

Union Pacific placed several additional orders for AC4400CWs starting in 1995, numbered in the 6700 and 6800 series, following former C&NW units that had been renumbered from the 8800 series following the merger in spring 1995. The UP eventually rostered more than 900 of the model including merger acquisitions.

6,000-hp diesels

Early in the development of AC traction, both builders envisioned single-engine 6,000-hp locomotives that could replace pairs of older 3,000-hp locomotives. Electro-Motive's SD90MAC-H and GE's AC6000CW were developed concurrently with this goal. The SD90MAC-H was built on an 80-foot 2-inch platform, riding on modern HTCR II trucks, with a Whisper Cab (acoustically isolated) and distinctive large radiators at the rear of the hood. Its defining technology was its pioneering

application of the GM16V265 four-cycle engine, a noteworthy departure from EMD's earlier engines that had used two-cycle designs.

For its AC6000CW, GE developed a new and significantly more-powerful engine in partnership with German manufacturer Deutz MWM. The result was what GE called the 7HDL, a V-type four-cycle diesel that operated at a maximum 1,050 rpm and put out 6,000 hp.

Union Pacific was a primary customer for both manufacturers' 6,000-hp locomotives. The railroad's traffic had grown in the mid-1990s, in part because of its acquisition of the Chicago & North Western and Southern Pacific systems, and UP wanted new locomotives as quickly as they could be delivered. Both GE and EMD broke with tradition by securing large orders for the new models prior to building fully functional prototypes. Both designs required longer developmental time than originally expected, so to meet UP's immediate need for motive power both builders offered similar compromise solutions by selling "upgradeable/convertible" locomotive platforms. The new locomotives were delivered with existing engine models of the lower horsepower rating, but designed to accept the new 6,000-hp engines when they were ready.

Electro-Motive's answer was the "upgradeable" SD9043MAC. It was delivered with the 16-710G3B engine rated at 4,300 hp, making it the functional equivalent of an SD70MAC. Union Pacific and Canadian Pacific were the primary customers for the SD9043MAC and the true 6,000-hp SD90MAC-H; UP acquired just over 300 of the 9043s beginning in 1995, then 60 of the true SD90MACs in 1998 and 2000.

GE called its locomotives "convertibles," with a 76-foot platform and the larger radiators required by the big engine—they were delivered, though, with GE's traditional 7FDL-16 engine rated at 4,400 hp, making them functionally AC4400CWs. In 1996, UP received the first of its convertible GEs (UP class C4460AC), eventually receiving just over 100, and in 1998 its true GE AC6000CWs (class C60AC), rostering 80.

Although UP was initially enthusiastic about the potential for 6,000-hp locomotives, both builders' models suffered

On April 2, 1980, UP SD40 No. 3028 leads Southern Pacific train MEWCM-02 (Medford to West Colton Manifest) past Harriman-era Union Switch & Signal Style B two-position, lower-quadrant semaphores at Ashland, Ore., on the Siskiyou Line. UP bought 135 SD40s from Electro-Motive in 1966; the last were off the roster by the end of 1992. *Don Marson*

The railroad had six 3,500-hp GP40X diesels, which rode on the unusual HT-B high-adhesion truck. In May 1988, Nos. 91 and 93 lead a westbound company business-car special over former Western Pacific trackage on Third Street in Oakland, Calif. The former Western Pacific Oakland station is at the left. *Don Marson*

from engine reliability issues compared to their lower-horsepower cousins. The railroad retained its upgradeable EMD units, but kept their 4,300-hp engines rather than swapping them out. Some of the SD90MAC-H diesels were retired, however, after just a few years of service. The UP had better luck with its 6,000-hp GEs, although it operated relatively few of them. Problems with GE's 6,000-hp engine led UP to downgrade the output of the AC6000CW by replacing the 6,000-hp 7HDL diesel with GE's most-modern 4,400-hp engine, reclassifying the locomotives C44ACCCA. Ultimately, UP returned to ordering more moderately powered 4,000- to 4,400-hp locomotives from both builders.

SD70M, SD70ACe, and SD70ACe-T4

In 1999 Union Pacific made an unusual decision—in that AC technology was available—to place an enormous order for EMD's DC-traction SD70M. The specifications for these locomotives represented a step back technologically, since they featured the older, simpler electrical system, incorporated a conventional control stand in place of the desktop style, and used mechanical fuel injection instead of computer-controlled electronic fuel injection. The decision was likely based on the reliability of the proven systems and the lower cost of DC- versus AC-traction locomotives. The UP would

For more than a quarter century the EMD SD40-2 was the mainstay of UP's road fleet. Ultimately UP rostered more than 1,200 of the type, including more than 680 that it bought new. Five SD40-2s roar east through Nevada's Clover Creek Canyon on March 4, 1997.
Brian Solomon

Westbound train ASKC (Alton & Southern to Kansas City), led by C30-7 No. 2436, crosses Livestock Drive at Gray Summit, Mo., on the evening of June 11, 1990. In the background is Purina Farms, an animal nutrition research farm established in 1926. *Scott Muskopf*

acquire more than a thousand of the model, built from 2000 to 2004 and numbered 3778 through 5221 (including 25 former SP SD70Ms). UP's later-built SD70Ms were powered by the emissions-compliant 16-710G3C-T1 engine.

In late 2003, EMD introduced a prototype SD70ACe, a modern diesel-electric that represented an advancement of its 1990s-era SD70MAC. It was powered by the 4,300-hp, EPA Tier 2-compliant 16-710G3C-T2 engine. Improvements promised higher reliability with longer intervals between required maintenance. It used fewer inverter components and reduced the number of electronic control cards from 50 to just two. The 710 engine was improved by lowering peak firing pressure, reducing stress and fatigue on primary components. Externally, the SD70ACe featured a new standard cab style, a variation used earlier on Union Pacific SD90MAC-H's a few years earlier. Interior ergonomics were improved by redesigning the desktop control layout.

New SD90MAC 8535 and two sisters rest at Belt Railway's Clearing yard in Chicago. Next to the true 6,000-hp units is SD9043MAC 8248, one of the "convertible" locomotives built with the older 4,300-hp 710 engine. The intended conversions never occurred, and the SD9043MACs operated as-built until retired. *Chris Guss*

On March 31, 1995, SD60 6051 leads a westbound freight through California's Afton Canyon at milepost 193.5 on the Los Angeles & Salt Lake route. In 1986, UP bought 85 SD60s, numbered in the 6000 block. They were joined by former Chicago & North Western SD60s in 1995. *Don Marson*

UP acquired more than 500 SD70ACes (Nos. 8309 to 8823). In addition, in 2014 UP ordered s variation of the SD70ACe ballasted four tons heavier per unit than the standard model to increase adhesion; these 281 locomotives were classified as SD70AH and numbered 8824 to 8996.

The weight precedent of those locomotives followed on orders for the more advanced SD70ACe-T4 models, which were designed to meet the latest Tier 4 air-quality standards. These were delivered beginning in 2016 and were classified as SD70AC-T4C. Some were numbered in the 3000 series (including three former demonstrators built in 2015), with others in the 8997-8104 block.

Heritage-scheme SD70ACes

In 2005, UP had six new SD70ACe diesels specially numbered and painted to commemorate its various merger partners of the 1980s and 1990s. Each scheme was designed to capture the spirit of the predecessors without directly replicating

On August 6, 2016, GE Tier 4-compliant ET44AH No. 2668 works as a tail-end DPU (distributed power unit) on an auto-rack train ascending the former SP grade in California's Tehachapis near Tunnel No. 2. The extra-large radiator at the back is a distinctive feature of GE's Tier 4 design.
Brian Solomon

their past schemes. Most of the road numbers reflected the year that the railroad was acquired by UP. They included Missouri Pacific (No. 1982), Western Pacific (No. 1983), Missouri-Kansas-Texas (No. 1988), Denver & Rio Grande Western (No. 1989, since since D&RGW's acquisition overlapped with other railroads' dates), Chicago & North Western (No. 1995), and Southern Pacific (No. 1996). Also specially adorned in 2005 was SD70Ace No. 8423, which was renumbered No. 4141 and painted in Air Force One colors to commemorate George H. W. Bush, America's 41st president.

EPA-compliant GE locomotives

Since the early 2000s, locomotive design has been driven largely by increasingly stringent emissions mandates. To comply with EPA Tier 2 requirements, which went into effect in 2005, GE re-engineered its electrical system and introduced the GEVO engine for its new Evolution Series locomotives. Union Pacific opted for GE's 4,400-hp, AC-traction ES44AC, as well as the more heavily ballasted ES44AH. Compared to earlier models, these required substantially thicker radiator "wings" (atop the end of the hood) to provide greater cooling capacity—a key to lowering emissions. To distinguish these Evolution-series models, UP classified them as C45ACCTE.

In the 2010s, GE made further design changes to meet tougher Tier 4 standards, which went into effect in 2015. GE replaced the existing single turbocharger with an innovative design using twin turbochargers operating sequentially. The smaller high-pressure turbocharger provides optimum performance at lower throttle positions, while the larger low-pressure unit is matched for higher-throttle positions. The more-

Union Pacific was the launch customer for Progress Rail's first Tier 4 road locomotive, model SD70ACe-T4, a type that was advanced from Electro-Motive's SD70MAC. This employed the new 1010J four-cycle diesel engine, which represented a distinct departure from the traditional EMD two-cycle engine first developed in the 1930s. UP initially assigned its SD70ACe-T4s to coal service. On April 17, 2017, Nos. 3025 and 3022 lead coal train CATOK9 21 at Shermer, Ill., (milepost 17.5) on UP's Milwaukee Subdivision where the line crosses Canadian Pacific's C&M Subdivision in the Chicago suburbs. *Chris Guss*

complicated cooling cycles also require substantially larger radiator assemblies—one of the principle external changes on Tier 4 models.

Union Pacific ordered GE's Tier 4 diesels starting in 2015 with the ET44AH (UP class C45AH), numbered starting in the 2520-series blocks. Many of UP's Tier 4 GE diesels were initially assigned to California and worked former Southern Pacific routes, including along what UP terms its "I-5 Corridor" between greater Los Angeles and the Pacific Northwest. In a press release, UP touted GE's Tier 4 locomotives, stating, "GE met the standard, producing a locomotive that ultimately reduces emissions by more than 70% versus their best Tier 3 (compliant) locomotive."

Classic-era switchers

Prior to its mergers in the 1980s and 1990s, UP operated hundreds of diesel-electric switching locomotives across its system. Most were standard models from various manufacurers, and most labored in relative obscurity compared to the railroad's fleets of high-profile road locomotives.

The railroad bought its first Electro-Motive switchers in October 1939, and ultimately rostered hundreds of end-cab NW2, SW7, SW9, and SW1200 models from that manufacturer. Among the more

DISTRIBUTED POWER

Union Pacific had experimented with radio-controlled remote helpers in the 1970s using specially outfitted SD40-2s, but the technology wasn't mature enough for widespread applications so the railroad discontinued these operations after just a few years. In 1995, UP reintroduced unmanned radio-controlled helpers, known in modern parlance as distributed power units or DPUs. General Electric was the driving force behind the successful application of DPUs. Many of UP's AC4400CWs were equipped with Locotrol III technology, a vastly improved radio system employed by GE that enabled an engineer to control up to four separate sets of locomotives.

In practice, UP operates two or three sets of DPUs in some trains. Distributing locomotives throughout a heavy train offers many operational advantages: it lowers drawbar stress, limits slack action, provides an engineer better train control, and aids in braking. DPU operation lowers costs by allowing much longer, heavier trains while eliminating the need for most manned helper districts. Today, distributed power is standard for the operation of heavy road freights on many lines across the system.

UP SD70ACe No. 4141 passes Mumford, Texas, with a Gulf Coast NRHS Chapter excursion on Nov. 20, 2005. This specially painted locomotive honors George H. W. Bush, the 41st president and railroad enthusiast, and emulates the paint scheme designed by Raymond Loewy worn by presidential aircraft. In 2019 the railroad donated No. 4141 to the George H. W. Bush Presidential Library & Museum in College Station, Texas for future display.
Tom Kline

The bell on the nose of Union Pacific GP50 No. 5518 gives away the locomotive's Chicago & North Western heritage. The C&NW was the only railroad that bought new locomotives with nose-mounted bells.
Scott Muskopf

The uniquely shaped herald of the Missouri-Kansas-Texas rides the flank of the nose of UP's M-K-T heritage locomotive SD70ACe No. 1988 leading an intermodal train through Lissie, Texas, on March 25, 2013. Note the HTCR-4 trucks. *Tom Kline*

unusual EMD switchers were eight two-unit "cow-calf" model TR5 transfer diesels (basically two SW9s, one cabless) designed for heavy yard work, which were also used as helpers on Cajon Pass. In the early 1980s, UP began rebuilding and upgrading many of its older EMD switchers, plus those acquired through merger from Missouri Pacific and Western Pacific. These rebuilds were reclassified as SW10s. Many remained on the roster until the late 1990s.

Among UP's early switchers were 100 Alco S models, mostly 1,000-hp S2s and S4s, plus a lone 600-hp S3 acquired in 1968 along with the Mount Hood Railway. A few of the Alcos were built with multiple-unit connections and were assigned to branchlines.

Especially rare were five Fairbanks-Morse H10-44 (1,000-hp) switchers bought between 1945 and 1947. Numbered 1300-1304, the F-Ms were originally dressed in utilitarian black paint.

Almost as rare were two types of Baldwin 1,000-hp switchers. The first to arrive were a half-dozen Baldwin VO1000s built during World War II and originally painted black with yellow lettering (with "Road of the Challengers" on the cab). These were followed by five DS4-4-1000s built in 1948. All of the F-Ms and Baldwins were retired in the 1960s.

Union Pacific also had a lone GE 44-tonner, bought in 1947 (No. 1399). It spent its first decade as the Omaha shop switcher before being transferred west, where it spent time at various yards. It was retired in the mid-1970s.

MK1200G

In the early 1990s, Morrison-Knudsen's MK Rail (which in 1999 became part of Wabtec's MotivePower Industries) engineered an experimental low-horsepower, low-emissions diesel switcher (model

MK1200G) that burned liquefied natural gas for fuel. Of the four built, Union Pacific leased two. After trial use in Salt Lake City, they were assigned to Los Angeles where emission reduction was a high priority. They operated on UP until mid-1998 when their lease expired. Afterward, the pair went to BNSF, which had already leased the other pair of LNG switchers.

Genset locomotives

The theory behind a genset locomotive is to save fuel and reduce emissions by employing multiple compact low-emission diesel engine/generator sets (up to four per locomotive) instead of a single large diesel engine and generator. The sets are computer synchronized to work efficiently with each other, automatically turning on and off as needed. Since each genset engine only runs when necessary, fuel consumption and exhaust emissions are both lower than a continuously running conventional diesel. The advantages promised by genset locomotives resulted in a variety of public-private partnerships.

Union Pacific was a genset pioneer, creating some of the fundamental technology used to produce them. In the early 2000s, public agencies offered funding assistance for UP to replace older diesels with new gensets to reduce emissions in densely populated areas. As a result, UP genset fleets were initially assigned to yards in California and Texas, two states with the most stringent emissions requirements.

The UP acquired its first genset in 2005, and by 2010 had 175 on its roster. This included 60 National Railway Equipment 3GS-21Bs (and a lone 2GS-14B), assigned to greater Los Angeles, 98 Railpower four-motor RP20BDs that were largely assigned

Days before the partial demolition of the Imperial Sugar plant at Sugar Land, Texas, a pair of General Electric Dash 8-40Bs scoot past the landmark structure on the way to Eagle Lake, Texas, on Dec. 16, 2010. The plant was once a big customer for Southern Pacific and later UP. *Tom Kline*

No. 2518 leads a local freight east of Council Bluffs, Iowa, on Aug. 25, 1998. In 1997, this unit was rebuilt by MPI at Boise, Idaho, from a former CSX GP40. It was downrated to 2,000 hp and redesignated GP38-3. In the early 2000s, UP renumbered the locomotive No. 1018. *Brian Solomon*

Storming out of Bakersfield, Calif., on April 1, 2007, Union Pacific SD70ACe heritage locomotive No. 1996 leads intermodal train ZBRLC 30. The Southern Pacific heritage locomotive was unveiled in August 2006. *Chris Guss*

On Jan. 20, 1996, UP No. 1818 leads the T&P local across the Huey P. Long Bridge in Baton Rouge, La. This span shouldn't be confused with the much larger bridge of the same name in New Orleans. No. 1818 is former Missouri Pacific GP38-2 898. *Brian Solomon*

around Fort Worth and Houston, and six-axle Railpower RP20CDs assigned to the former SP Roseville (Calif.) Yard.

Unfortunately, the heyday of UP's genset locomotives was comparatively short. They suffered from various mechanical and reliability issues that negated any savings or emissions benefits. The railroad's official word on them: "Gensets served as a bridge technology to reduce emissions, although reliability and maintenance challenges prevented their greater adoption." UP's last gensets were acquired in 2010, and by 2018 the railroad was retiring or selling them.

Merger acquisitions

Union Pacific's diesel fleet grew rapidly during the 1980s and 1990s as a result of mergers. In addition to common models such as GP38-2s and SD40-2 that UP already owned, the railroad also inherited many models that it hadn't previously rostered, while adding collections of older models that it had once operated but since cleared from the roster.

Among locomotives acquired from Missouri Pacific were EMD GP15-1s and GP15ACs, GP18s, GP28s, GP35s, GP38s, GP38-2s, GP50s, SW1500s, MP15s, SD40s, and SD40-2s, plus General Electric U23Bs, U30Cs, B23-7s, and B30-7s. Western Pacific contributed numerous EMDs, among them a pair of F7As (never renumbered), GP7s, GP9s, GP20s, GP35s, GP40s, and GP40-2s, plus a handful of switchers including an SW1, SW9s, SW1500s, along with GE U23B and U30B road diesels.

Katy's roster of diesels added relatively few new locomotives to UP's fleet, but included many older four-axle models, among them GP38s, GP38-2s, GP38ACs, GP39-2s, and GP40s (some recently bought from Conrail), along with 36 SD40-2s plus SW1500 and MP15AC switchers. Katy's oldest units—GP7s, an F3Am, and a half-dozen RS3Ms—were never assigned UP numbers.

In 1995 Chicago & North Western contributed more than 775 locomotives to UP's fleet, including nearly new GE Dash 9s and AC4400CWs as well as modern Dash 8-40Cs and EMD SD60s. Along with this modern power came a variety of older

In the 1980s, UP rebuilt a number of older Electro-Motive switchers, assigning them the "SW10" designation. No. 1270, here at Portland, Ore., in 1985, was originally Missouri Pacific SW9 No. 1233, which had been rebuilt in 1984. UP sold off most its SW10s in the late 1990s; this one left the roster in 1997. *Dan Howard*

EMDs, among them several rebuilt GP7s (designated GP9R)—many originally built for the Rock Island—largely assigned to branch lines. The C&NW also contributed GP15-1s, GP38-2s, GP40s, GP50s, SD18s, SD40-2s, more than a dozen SD45s, 35 SD50s, and some MP15s, plus four F7As and three F7Bs—some of which had been reserved for C&NW's executive train—which were later transferred to UP's heritage fleet.

The Southern Pacific merger created by far the largest change to UP's locomotive fleet by adding more than 2,100 units to the roster. At the merger, many SP locomotives still wore Rio Grande paint and numbers; many others were painted in SP's scarlet and gray but were lettered for its Cotton Belt subsidiary.

Among the most distinctive acquisitions were SP's tunnel-motor, 1970s-built SD45T-2 and SD40T-2 diesels, which had unique low-level screened radiator air intakes at the ends of their long hoods. This was done to improve engine performance by pulling in cooler air at lower levels in tunnels, hence the nickname.

Beginning in the late 1960s, SP embarked on a large-scale program to rebuild and upgrade its older diesels to modern standards, with most work done at its Sacramento (Calif.) shops. Most received updated model designations using an E or R suffix to reflect rebuilt status. These included large numbers of overhauled 1950s-era GP9Es, SD7Es, and SD9Es, as well as GP20Rs, GP35Rs, SD35Rs, SD40Rs, and SD45Rs. The SP also had many newer or un-rebuilt locomotives including SD38s and SD39s, high-horsepower, four-motor GP40s, GP40Ps, a lone GP40X, and GP40-2s, and relatively new GP60s, along with fleets of substantially rebuilt GP40Ms and SD40Ms acquired by SP during its power-short years in the early 1990s.

The SP had been one of GE's best customers and operated fleets of B23-7s, B30-7s, B36-7s, B39-8s and Dash 8-40Bs. SP's newest locomotives included a fleet of 25 SD70Ms, 101 Dash 9-44s, and 277 AC4400CWs that fit in well with UP's own recent new locomotives. The SP also had hundreds of switchers, mostly SW1500s,

This Railpower model RP20SD is a three-genset, six-motor locomotive. This type was built on recycled Missouri Pacific SD40 platforms. In May 2008, UP displayed brand-new UPY No. Y896 at the California State Railroad Museum in Sacramento, Calif., before it was assigned to hump service at Roseville, Calif. Units wearing UPY (Union Pacific Yard) numbers represent a distinct fleet from UP's road diesels. *Brian Solomon*

MP15ACs, and MP15DCs. Among the Rio Grande antiques inherited by UP were unmodified GP30s, which largely remained in former D&RGW territory for several years under UP control. Other former Rio Grande locomotives included GP40s, GP40-2s, GP60s, SD40T-2s, SD45s, SD50s, and SW1000 and SW1200 switchers.

Some incoming locomotives were retired immediately or operated briefly and then sold or retired before being repainted; most were repainted and renumbered to the UP fleet. Many can be spotted by their detail variations compared to original UP locomotives. As can be imagined, the influx of additional locomotives—on top of seven decades of UP's own diesel purchases and retirements—made renumbering extremely complex.

Eye on the future

In January 2022, Union Pacific announced that it planned to acquire 20 innovative battery-electric locomotives, investing in models from both Progress Rail and Wabtec, the locomotive builders that respectively inherited the legacies of Electro-Motive and General Electric. The battery-electrics are expected to be delivered during 2023 and 2024 and initially tested in yard service. Lance Fritz, UP's chairman, president and CEO as of 2022, is optimistic about the new technology, saying, "We're committed to actions that reduce Union Pacific's environmental footprint as we work toward our ultimate goal of reaching net zero emissions by 2050."

BIBLIOGRAPHY

BOOKS

Encyclopedia of American Business History and Biography: Railroads in the Nineteenth Century. Bruccoli Clark Layman, Inc., and Facts on File, Inc. 1988.

The American Railway—Its Construction, Development, Management, and Appliances. New York, 1893

Asay, Jeff S. *Track and Time—an Operational History of the Western Pacific Railroad through Timetables and Maps.* Portola, Calif., 2006.

Austin, Ed and Tom Dill. *The Southern Pacific in Oregon.* Edmonds, Wash., 1987.

Baedeker, Karl. *Baedeker's The United States—Handbook for Travelers.* Leipzig: Karl Baedeker Publishing, 1909

Bancroft, Hubert Howe. *History of California, Vol. VII.* San Francisco, 1890.

Beebe, Lucius. *The Central Pacific and the Southern Pacific Railroads.* Berkeley, Calif. 1963.

————. *The Overland Limited.* Berkeley, Calif. 1963.

Beebe, Lucius, and Charles Clegg. *Narrow Gauge in the Rockies.* Berkeley, Calif., 1958.

Bruce, Alfred W. *The Steam Locomotive in America.* New York, 1952.

Bryant, Keith L. *History of the Atchison, Topeka and Santa Fe Railway.* New York, 1974.

Bryant, Jr., Keith L. *Railroads in the Age of Regulation, 1900-1980.* New York, 1988.

Bush, Donald, J. *The Streamlined Decade.* New York, 1975.

Chernow, Ron. *The House of Morgan.* New York, 1990.

Churella, Albert, J. *From Steam to Diesel.* Princeton, N.J. 1998.

Conrad, J. David. *The Steam Locomotive Directory of North America.* Vols. I & II. Polo, Ill.: Transportation Trails, 1988.

Cudahy, Brian J. *Box Boats.* New York, 2006.

Daggett, Stuart. *History of the Southern Pacific.* New York, 1922.

DeBoer, David J. *Piggyback and Containers.* San Marino, Calif., Golden West Books, 1992.

DeNevi, Don. *The Western Pacific—Railroading Yesterday, Today and Tomorrow.* Seattle, Wash., 1978.

Doherty, Timothy Scott, and Brian Solomon. *Conrail.* MBI Publishing, St. Paul, Minn., 2004.

Dorin, Patrick C. and Robert C. Del Grosso. *Burlington Northern Railroad: Coal Hauler and Coal Country Trackside Guide.* Bonners Ferry, Idaho, 1995.

Dorsey, Edward Bates. *English and American Railroads Compared.* New York, 1887.

Droege, John A. *Freight Terminals and Trains.* New York, 1912.

————. *Passenger Terminals and Trains.* New York, 1916.

Drury, George H. *The Historical Guide to North American Railroads.* Waukesha, Wis., 1985.

————. *The Train Watcher's Guide to North American Railroads.* Waukesha, Wis., 1992.

————. *Guide to North American Steam Locomotives.* Waukesha, Wis., 1993.

Dubin, Arthur D. *Some Classic Trains.* Milwaukee, Wis. 1964.

Dubin, Arthur D. *More Classic Trains.* Milwaukee, Wis. 1974.

Duke, Donald. *Union Pacific in Southern California 1890-1990.* San Marino, Calif., 2005.

Dunscomb, Guy, L. *A Century of Southern Pacific Steam Locomotives.* Modesto, Calif., 1963.

Farrington, Jr., S. Kip. *Railroading from the Head End.* New York, 1943.

————. *Railroads at War.* New York, 1944.

————. *Railroading from the Rear End.* New York, 1946.

————. *Railroads of Today.* New York, 1949.

————. *Railroading the Modern Way.* New York, 1951.

————. *Railroads of the Hour.* New York, 1958.

————. *Railroading Coast to Coast.* New York, 1976.

Frey, Robert L. *Railroads in the Nineteenth Century.* New York, 1988.

Garmany, John B. *Southern Pacific Dieselization.* Edmonds, Wash., 1985.

Grodinsky, Julius. *Jay Gould—His Business Career 1867-1892.* Philadelphia, 1957.

Gruber, John. *Railroad History in a Nutshell.* Madison, Wis., 2009

————. *Railroad Preservation in a Nutshell.* Madison, Wis., 2011

Gruber, John, and Brian Solomon. *The Milwaukee Road's HIAWATHAS.* St. Paul, Minn., 2006.

Hayes, William Edward. *Iron Road to Empire—The History of the Rock Island Lines.* 1953.

Heath, Erle. *Seventy-Five Years of Progress—Historical Sketch of the Southern Pacific.* San Francisco, 1945.

Hedges, James Blaine. *Henry Villard and the Railways of the Northwest.* New York, 1930.

Hidy, Ralph W., and Muriel E. Hidy, Roy V. Scott, with Don L. Hofsommer. *The Great Northern Railway.* Boston, 1988.

Hilton, George W. *American Narrow Gauge Railroads.* Stanford, Calif., 1990.

Holbrook, Stewart H. *The Story of American Railroads.* New York, 1947.

————. *James J. Hill.* New York, 1955.

Holland, Rupert Sargent. *Historic Railroads.* Philadelphia, 1927.

Hofsommer, Don. L. *Southern Pacific 1900-1985.* College Station, Texas, 1986.

Hollander, Stanley, C. *Passenger Transportation.* Lansing, Mich. 1968.

Jennison, Brian and Victor Neves. *Southern Pacific Oregon Division.* Mukilteo, Wash., 1997.

Johnson, Emory, R. *American Railway Transportation.* New York, 1910.

Keilty, Edmund. *Interurbans Without Wires.* Glendale, Calif., 1979.

Kirkland, John, F. *Dawn of the Diesel Age.* Pasadena, Calif., 1994.

Kirkland, John, F. *The Diesel Builders* Vols. I, II, and III. Glendale, Calif., 1983.

Klein, Maury. *History of the Louisville & Nashville Railroad.* New York, 1972.

————. *Union Pacific*, Vols. I &II. New York, 1989.

————. *Union Pacific: The Reconfiguration; American's Greatest Railroad from 1969 to the Present.* Oxford, New York, 2011.

Kratville, William, and Harold E. Ranks. *Motive Power of the Union Pacific.* Omaha, Neb., 1958.

Latham, Earl. *The Politics of Railroad Coordination 1933-1936.* Cambridge, Mass., 1959

LeMassena, Robert A. *Colorado's Mountain Railroads.* Golden, Colo., 1963.

————. *Rio Grande to the Pacific.* Denver, 1974

Lewis, Oscar. *The Big Four.* New York, 1938.

Malone, Michael P. James J. Hill, *Empire Builder of the Northwest.* Norman, Okla., 1996.

Marre, Louis A. and Jerry A. Pinkepank. *The Contemporary Diesel Spotter's Guide.* Milwaukee, Wis., 1985.

Marre, Louis, A. *Diesel Locomotives: The First 50 Years.* Waukesha, Wis., 1995.

Marre, Louis A. and Paul K. Withers. *The Contemporary Diesel Spotter's Guide*, Year 2000 Edition. Halifax, Pa., 2000.

Marshall, James. *Santa Fe—The Rail-*

road That Built an Empire. New York, 1945.

McDonald, Charles W. *Diesel Locomotive Rosters*. Milwaukee, Wis., 1982.

McDonnell, Greg. *U-Boats: General Electric Diesel Locomotives*, Toronto, 1994.

Middleton, William D. *Landmarks on the Iron Road*. Bloomington, Ind., 1999.

Middleton, William D. with George M. Smerk, and Roberta L. Diehl. *Encyclopedia of North American Railroads*. Indiana University Press, Bloomington and Indianapolis, 2007.

Miner, Craig H. *The St. Louis-San Francisco Transcontinental Railroad*. Lawrence, Kans., 1972.

————. *The Rebirth of the Missouri Pacific, 1956-1983*. College Station, Texas, 1983.

Myrick, David F. *Life and Times of the Central Pacific Railroad*. Book Club of California, 1969.

————. *Western Pacific—The Last Transcontinental Railroad*. Colorado Rail Annual No. 27. Colorado, 2006.

Overton, Richard, C. *Burlington West*. Cambridge, Mass., 1941.

————. *Burlington Route*. New York, 1965.

Pinkepank, Jerry A. *The Diesel Spotter's Guide*. Milwaukee, Wis., 1967.

Potter, Janet Greenstein. *Great American Railroad Stations*. New York, 1996.

Quiett, Glenn Chesney. *They Built the West*. New York, 1934.

Ransome-Wallis, P. *World Railway Locomotives*. New York, 1959.

Reck, Franklin M. *On Time*. Electro-Motive Division of General Motors, 1948.

Reck, Franklin M. *The Dilworth Story*. New York, 1954.

Reed, S. G. *A History of the Texas Railroads*. Houston, Texas. 1941.

Riegel, Robert Edgar. *The Story of the Western Railroads*. Lincoln, Neb., 1926.

Ryan, Dennis and Joseph Shine. *Southern Pacific Passenger Trains*. Vols.1& 2. La Mirada, Calif., 1986, 2000.

Saunders, Richard, Jr. *The Railroad Mergers and the Coming of Conrail*. Westport, Conn. 1978.

————. *Merging Lines: American Railroads 1900-1970*. DeKalb, Ill., 2001.

————. *Main Lines: American Railroads 1970-2002*. DeKalb, Ill., 2003.

Schafer, Mike with Joe Walsh. *Classic American Streamliners*. Osceola, Wis., 1997.

Shearer, Frederick. E. *The Pacific Tourist*. New York, 1970.

Signor, John R. *Beaumont Hill*. San Marino, Calif. 1990.

————. *Donner Pass: Southern Pacific's Sierra Crossing*. San Marino, Calif. 1985.

————. *Rails in the Shadow of Mt. Shasta*. San Diego, 1982.

————. *Southern Pacific's Coast Line*. Wilton, Calif., 1994.

————. *Tehachapi*. San Marino, Calif. 1983.

————. *Western Division*. Wilton, Calif., 2003

Smalley, Eugene V. *History of the Northern Pacific Railroad*. New York, 1883.

Solomon, Brian. *Trains of the Old West*. New York, 1998.

————. *The American Steam Locomotive*. Osceola, Wis., 1998.

————. *Southern Pacific Railroad*. Osceola, Wis., 1999.

————. *The American Diesel Locomotive*. Osceola, Wis., 2000.

————. *Super Steam Locomotives*. Osceola, Wis., 2000.

————. *Locomotive*. Osceola, Wis., 2001.

————. *Railway Masterpieces: Celebrating the World's Greatest Trains, Stations and Feats of Engineering*. Iola, Wisconsin, 2002.

————. *GE Locomotives*. St. Paul, Mn., 2003.

————. *Railroad Signaling*. St. Paul, Minn., 2003.

————. *Burlington Northern Santa Fe Railway*. St. Paul, Minn., 2005.

————. *Southern Pacific Passenger Trains*. St. Paul, Minn., 2005.

————. *EMD Locomotives*. St. Paul, Minn., 2006.

————. *Railroads of California*. Voyageur Press. Minneapolis, Minn., 2009.

————. *Alco Locomotives.* Voyageur Press. Minneapolis, Minn., 2009.

————. *Baldwin Locomotives.* Voyageur Press. Minneapolis, Minn., 2010.

————. *Electro-Motive E-Units and F-Units*. St. Paul, Minn., 2011.

————. *North American Railroad—the Illustrated Encyclopedia*. Voyageur Press. Minneapolis, Minn., 2012.

Staff, Virgil. *D-Day on the Western Pacific*. Glendale, Calif., 1982.

Staufer, Alvin F. and Edward L. May. *New York Central's Later Power*. Medina, Ohio, 1981

Starr, John W. *One Hundred Years of American Railroading*. Millersburg, Pa., 1927.

Steinbrenner, Richard T. *The American Locomotive Company—A Centennial Remembrance*. Warren, New Jersey, 2003.

Stover, John F. *The Life and Decline of the American Railroad*. New York, 1970.

————. *History of the New York Central Railroad*. New York, 1975.

————. *The Routledge Historical Atlas of the American Railroads*. New York, 1999.

Strapac, Joseph A. *Southern Pacific Review 1952-1982*. Huntington Beach, Calif., 1983.

————. *Southern Pacific Review 1953-1985*. Huntington Beach, Calif., 1986

————. *Southern Pacific Historic Diesels,* Vols. 3-10. Huntington Beach, Calif., and Bellflower, Calif., 2003

————. *Southern Pacific Motive Power Annuals,* 1967-1968, 1970, 1971, 1972. Burlingame, Calif., 1968 to 1972.

Strack, Don. *Union Pacific 2000—Locomotive Directory*. Halifax, Pa., 2000.

Swengel, Frank M. *The American Steam Locomotive: Volume 1, Evolution*. Davenport, Iowa, 1967.

Thompson, Gregory Lee. *The Passenger Train in the Motor Age*. Columbus, Ohio, 1993.

Vance, Jr., James E. *The North American Railroad*. Baltimore, 1995.

Walker, Mike. *Steam Powered Video's Comprehensive Railroad Atlas of North America—North East U.S.A*. Steam Powered Publishing. Feaversham, Kent, UK, 1993.

————. *California and Nevada*. Feaversham, Kent, UK, 1996

————. *Great Lakes West*. Feaversham, Kent, UK, 1996

————. *Great Lakes East*. Feaversham, Kent, UK, 1997

————. *Pacific Northwest*. Feaversham, Kent, UK, 1997

————. *Mountain Plains*. Feaversham, Kent, UK, 2000

————. *Texas*. Feaversham, Kent, UK, 2001

White, John H. Jr. *A History of the American Locomotive—Its Development: 1830-1880*. Baltimore, 1968.

————. *The American Railroad Passenger Car*, Vols. I & II. Baltimore, 1978.

————. *Early American Locomotives*. Toronto, 1979.

Wilson, Neill C., and Frank J. Taylor *Southern Pacific: The Roaring Story of a Fighting Railroad*. New York, 1952.

Wilson, O. Meredith. *The Denver and Rio Grande Project, 1870-1901*. Salt Lake City, 1982.

Winchester, Clarence. *Railway Wonders of the World*, Vols. 1 & 2. London, 1935.

Wright, Richard K. *Southern Pacific Daylight*. Thousand Oaks, Calif., 1970.

PERIODICALS

American Railroad Journal and Mechanics' Magazine. (Published in the 1830s and 1840s)

Baldwin Locomotives. Philadelphia, Pa. (no longer published)

Classic Trains. Waukesha, Wis.

Diesel Era. Halifax, Pa.

CTC Board. Ferndale, Washington

Diesel Railway Traction, supplement to *Railway Gazette* (UK). (merged into *Railway Gazette*).

Extra 2200 South. Cincinnati, Ohio. (no longer published)

Jane's World Railways. London.

Moody's Analyses of Investments, Part I—Steam Railroads. New York.

Pacific RailNews. Waukesha, Wis. (no longer published)

Railroad History, formerly *Railway and Locomotive Historical Society Bulletin*. Boston, Mass.

Official Guide to the Railways. New York

Railway and Locomotive Engineering. New York. (no longer published)

Railway Age. Chicago and New York.

Railway Gazette, 1870-1908. New York. (no longer published)

San Francisco Chronicle. San Francisco.

Southern Pacific Bulletin. San Francisco. (no longer published)

The Railway Gazette. London.

Trains. Waukesha, Wis.

Vintage Rails. Waukesha, Wis. (no longer published)

Washington Post. Washington D.C.

BROCHURES, TIMETABLES, RULE BOOKS, AND REPORTS

Baldwin Locomotive Works. 6,000 H.P Diesel Electric Road Freight Locomotives. Philadelphia, 1949.

Bearce, W.D. *Steam-Electric Locomotive*. Erie, Pa. 1939.

Chicago Operating Rules Association, *Operating Guide*, 1994

Finance Docket No. 32760, Railroad Merger Application, Vol. 3. (UP-SP operating plan), 1995.

General Code of Operating Rules, Fourth Edition. 2000.

General Electric. Achieving a leadership position in turbocharger technology. Erie, Pa., 1982

General Electric. A New Generation For Increased Productivity. Erie, Pa., 1987

General Electric. GE Diesel Engines—Power for Progress. Erie, Pa., 1988

General Motors. Electro-Motive Division Operating Manual No. 2300. La Grange, Ill., 1945.

Interstate Commerce Commission. Fourth Annual Report on the Statistics of Railways of the United States for the year ended June 30, 1891. Washington, D.C. 1892

Southern Pacific Company. Pacific System Time Table No. 17, Coast Division. 1896.

Southern Pacific Company. Public timetables, 1930 to 1958

Southern Pacific. *Your Daylight Trip*. 1939.

Southern Pacific Lines. Western Region Timetable 3. 1989.

Union Pacific Railroad Company. Public timetables, 1957 to 1969

Union Pacific Railroad Company. System and Area timetables, 1990 to 2011.

United States Patents:

809,974. Jan 16, 1906. W. R. McKeen, Jr.

809,974. Jan 16, 1906. W. R. McKeen, Jr.

972,467. October 11, 1910. W. R. McKeen, Jr.

972,502. October 25, 1910. E.H. Harriman and W. R. McKeen, Jr.

973,622. October 25, 1910. E. G. Budd.

2,079,748. May 11, 1937. Martin Blomberg.

2,247,273. June 24, 1941. Martin Blomberg.

INTERNET SOURCES

rrpicturearchives.net (Railroad Picture Archives)

utahrails.net (Utah Rails)

www.aar.org (Association of American Railroads)

www.ble.orgx (Brotherhood of Locomotive Engineers)

www.bnsf.com (BNSF Railway)

www.fra.dot.gov (Federal Railroad Administration)

www.gwrr.com (Genesee & Wyoming)

www.uprr.com (Union Pacific)

LEGENDARY LOCOMOTIVES!

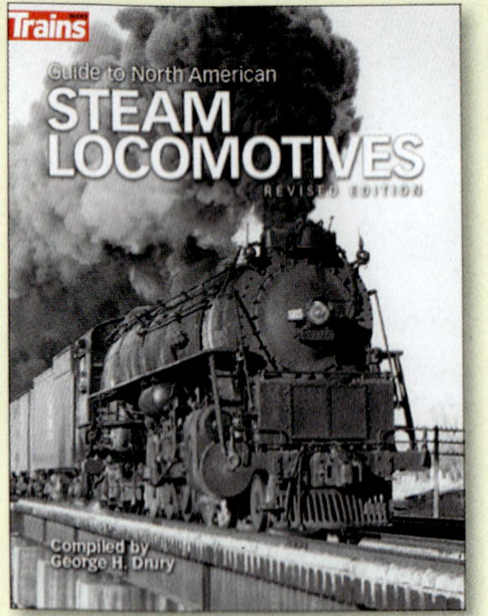

This newly revamped book features every steam locomotive built in the U.S., Mexico, and Canada since 1900. This is an essential guide that should be in the library of every railfan! It includes comprehensive rosters for every railroad. Plus Information and data railfans can't find anywhere else.

Item #01302 • $27.99

This updated encyclopedia of railroading presents history, photos, route maps, and fast facts for 170+ North American railroads. A new, searchable index makes locating information easy and fast. Learn about railroad lines that were abandoned or merged, and more!

Item #01117 • $24.99

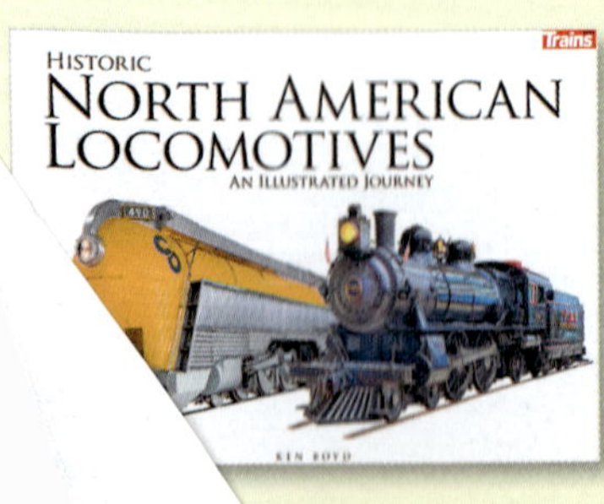

This museum-quality book traces the development of North American locomotives from the early 1800s to the present. The collection presents 100 locomotives that are rarely shown together in the same book. Features include detailed and colored photographs created through painterly techniques, and more!

$29.99

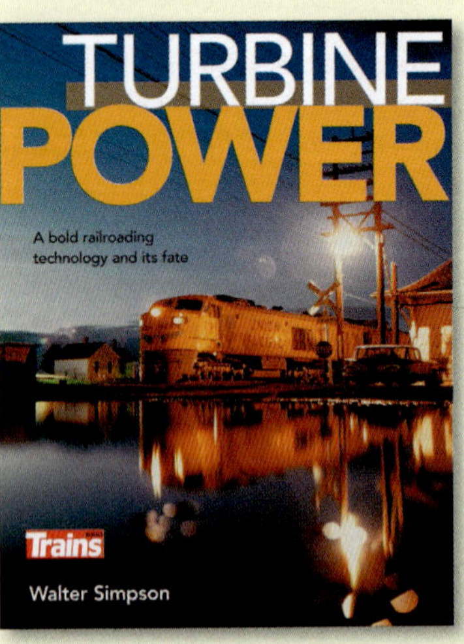

This is the first book that brings together information about turbine locomotives and trains that collects all of the various projects in one place. From first prototypes to the most recent proposals, everything is presented with vintage images and references that all railroad fans will enjoy.

Item #01310 • $22.99

207

ow from your local hobby shop or at KalmbachHobbyStore.com